Adopting Alesia

My Crusade for My Russian Daughter

by Dee Thompson

Keep the faith!
Love
Dee Thompson

Scribblerchick
Books   A Wyatt-MacKenzie
IMPRINT

Adopting Alesia
My Crusade for My Russian Daughter

by Dee Thompson

Scribblerchick Books
an imprint of

Wyatt-MacKenzie Publishing
For Imprint information visit: www.WyMacPublishing.com

Requests for permission or further information should be addressed to:
Wyatt-MacKenzie Publishing, 15115 Highway 36,
Deadwood, Oregon 97430

TABLE OF CONTENTS

Dedication

To My Lovely, Amazing Daughter
Alesia, the light of my life

Introduction

When I was a little girl, I always assumed that I would get married and have children after I finished college. As I got older, I developed a timetable. By the time I was twenty-eight, I was supposed to be married and have my first child. By thirty-two, child number two would appear. I would stay at home and be a full-time mom and part-time writer.

Of course, life never turns out like you think it will. Sometime around my late twenties, I realized that the plan wasn't really working out. I decided that if I was not a wife and mother by age thirty-five, I would look into having a child on my own.

My father died from cancer when I was 34, and for the next couple of years, I lived in a haze of grief and unformed plans and ideas, coping as well as I could. I vaguely realized that my time to become a mother was slipping by, but it took until I was 38 to find a job I liked where I didn't feel terribly stressed all the time. Even then, I somehow couldn't quite bring myself to start trying to have a child. It just seemed wrong without a husband. I dated a lot of guys, but none was The One.

By the age of forty, I was doing okay financially, even though being a paralegal isn't terribly lucrative. I owned a condo and had a nice car and reasonably decent job. I had been to Europe.

But I had no husband and no children—just a string of relationships that hadn't worked out and a rising sense of panic about having missed my chance (biologically) to become a mother. I pondered options. I could find the first man who seemed decent and marry him, but the old aphorism kept echoing in my head, "Marry in haste, repent in leisure." I could do artificial insemination. That seemed expensive and complicated, and I didn't relish the thought of being pregnant and alone. Or I could adopt. That seemed way too difficult and complicated, and I wasn't sure that a single woman *could* adopt.

I started dating a new man around that time. He was dear and I loved being with him, but I couldn't really hope for a long-term relationship. He had gone through a painful breakup and refused to consider anything serious with me. We saw each other casually and I tried to accept things, though it was difficult emotionally.

I was depressed about my situation. I had no children to love. I wanted a family more than anything else in the world. I asked God for a miracle. (I didn't really expect a miracle, but figured it wouldn't hurt to ask.) But, in an amazing way that astonishes me to this day, God answered. And His answer was "Yes." At the end of a remarkable two-year journey, I was the proud and scared first-time mom of a beautiful thirteen year-old girl, Alesia.

Some looked at me aghast when I told them I was adopting an older child. A few actually shook their heads in horror. *She will be a behavior problem*, they said. *She will be a huge burden*, they said. *Russian?! She will have FAS (fetal alcohol syndrome).* I kept hearing, "You don't know what you're getting into, Dee! How will you cope?" They were gripped by fear for me and I understood it. But it didn't deter me.

I listened and answered them in this way: I wanted to have a child, and she needed a mother. It couldn't be more simple or right than that. "Sure," I said, "there will be challenges. There are always challenges with biological children, too."

The journey to get Alesia taught me a great deal. I found I could overcome huge obstacles and be emotionally strong. It taught me that even though I was single, I could make my own family and be a mother.

Throughout the ordeal, the only thing that mattered was

Alesia. I felt delighted about her throughout the adoption process. I got to know her through her letters. I felt blessed because I knew I would be getting a wonderful daughter.

I had always believed in God, but the adoption was a real test of my beliefs. Despite the many obstacles—or in retrospect, maybe because of them—by going through the adoption process, I gained a much deeper trust in God. It became a true journey of faith.

This is the story of that remarkable journey.

Chapter One

TO RUSSIA AND BACK

You would not think, from my history, that I would grow up to have a very unconventional family. I was raised by a conservative Republican father and a stay-at-home mother. We lived in the suburbs and were middle class. I took piano lessons. We took vacations at the beach. We had a dog and a cat. My older brother Bruce and I went to public schools.

However typical my childhood may have appeared on the surface, we were actually a somewhat unusual family. I was raised by two people with genius level IQ's and highly original and hysterical comic abilities. Mom and Dad would tell amazing stories. My mother was a professional singer when she was young, and I inherited her voice and some of her talent. My father loved history and passed that lifelong love to me. He also loved movies—we saw a lot of them. (I was almost born in a theater showing *High Noon*. Mom was in labor but Dad hated to leave early.)

I grew up with a passion for the theatre. I worked backstage or acted in a lot of plays in high school and got a degree in drama from the University of Georgia, thinking I wanted to be a playwright, if the singing didn't work out. I had nothing to write about in college. I remember thinking, age 20, I can't write yet because nothing interesting has happened to me!

Like many drama majors, I couldn't find a job after I graduated from college. I worked part-time in a bookstore for a while. Then my father talked me into going to paralegal school in Atlanta, and voilá, I became a paralegal in only ninety days.

I moved back to Knoxville and got a job. I decided the singing career would be too hard and wondered about my other dream, to become a writer—how to find the time to write and be a paralegal, too. It was still tough to think about what to write. And I couldn't afford a computer.

I went back to school part-time in 1987 and finished an M.A. in creative writing in 1990. I started writing seriously then, mostly poetry and stories. I finally had some life experiences that prepared me (or so I thought). Eventually I turned to screenwriting, but I was never very good at screenplays.

In 1993, I moved to Atlanta, where I've been ever since. I love Atlanta—the weather is great, most folks are nice, and my friends and family are either here or close.

I dated, but again couldn't seem to find The One. My weight bounced up and down because I am an emotional eater. That didn't help the dating situation. Writing became a refuge. As I neared 40, I was restless.

On the 4th of July, 2002, my cousin and friend Steve Embry took me out to lunch for my fortieth birthday. We went to my favorite Chinese restaurant (near the train station), where I am usually the only non-Asian person. I had garlic chicken and the best eggrolls in Atlanta. I recall it clearly because it was a momentous birthday.

Steve told me he was excited about being part of a new choir. It had been organized by the Baptist International Missions Board to fly to Khabarovsk, Russia (in far eastern Russia, on the edge of Siberia) and perform Handel's *Messiah* with the Khabarovsk symphony—the first time it had ever been performed in Siberia. After he finished, I laughed and told him he was crazy to go to Siberia in January. I kept to myself the fact that I was somewhat envious of his trip.

My interest in Russia had started early. In 1972, my parents, brother and I had seen a movie called *Nicholas and Alexandra*, about the last Tsar of Russia. Though at the time I was only ten years old, I was fascinated. A few years later, I read the book on which the movie was based and became fascinated by all things Russian.

In the weeks following that fateful lunch, Steve asked me to help him learn the *Messiah*. The choir was composed of people from all over America, and there would only be time for a few rehearsals. Most choir members knew the *Messiah* well, but Steve was a novice singer. I had sung it many times. As we talked about it and I helped him with his voice training, I began to envy his adventure even more. I had not sung in a regular choir in years, and I missed the experience.

When I was younger, I had done a lot of singing in school and church choirs, studying voice for five years. My first voice teacher was bitterly disappointed that I didn't want to pursue a career in opera. I had the voice for it perhaps, but not the vision. I just liked to sing because it was exhilarating.

In September, Steve finally suggested that I join the choir. I am not Baptist, but that didn't really make a difference. I am a Christian. I love the *Messiah*... After a lot of thought, I decided to go for it, and I signed on.

I had no idea how much my life was about to change.

The choir was mainly composed of folks from all over the southeast. Many had sung before in large church choirs and several were directors of music for their churches. It was a very talented group.

I was one of only a few sopranos—not many women wanted to go to Siberia in January. It made for a nerve-wracking rehearsal process. We were challenged to be heard against more than six strong basses, and more than eight altos. But I have a big voice and I sang my heart out. We had only two rehearsals in Atlanta before the trip.

I worked for a hotel company and so had easy access to maps. I located a large, laminated map of the world and hung it in my cubicle. I suddenly became fascinated with geography. I looked at Europe, where I had spent part of one summer, and then looked to the right of it. *Wow,* I thought, *Russia is huge!* Moscow is east of Frankfurt. There are a number of cities in western Russia. Then I looked to the right and there was Siberia—a vast area, with very few cities, though it is larger geographically than the USA. Finally, in the far right just above China, was Khabarovsk territory. I found Vladivostock and looked up. There was the city of Khabarovsk. I looked back at the USA. Russia appeared to be a huge and fascinating place, dwarfing the USA in comparison.

Emotionally, I looked forward to the trip because I needed a challenge. I was forty years old and I was tired—of looking for *Mr. Right,* of my job as a paralegal. I tried not to mourn the loss of the dream of having a family, but I felt a deep sense of sadness. I instinctively felt that I needed a change in my life and I somehow knew the choir trip would provide it. I would be right beyond my wildest dreams.

First of all, Russia itself was an amazing experience. I had been to Germany, France, and England, but never anywhere as exotic as Russia. We spent the first couple of days of our trip in Moscow. It's an enormous city. You see apartment buildings everywhere—huge drab-colored, blocky buildings, each holding thousands of apartments. There are tacky commercial buildings lit with neon, intermixed with gorgeous eighteenth century buildings that look like they indeed belong to another time. The people dress fashionably, wear a lot of dark colors, and rarely smile. Traffic is horrific and scary—even for someone from Atlanta. Nobody obeys traffic or parking laws.

When we arrived in Moscow, we all slept like the dead. The huge American style hotel was luxurious but stank of cigarette smoke. It was arranged that a translator and guide would accompany us on a bus that carried us over the wide streets of Moscow, and the following day, we were treated to a visit to the Kremlin and the Armoury. Though I was jet-lagged, I was fascinated.

The Kremlin is actually a collection of buildings—not just one big one, as most people think—made up of several churches and government buildings. We took a quick turn through the Armoury, which is a museum. It houses unbelievable Tsarist treasures—Fabergé eggs, the coronation robes of tsars, gifts to the royal family from ambassadors, suits of armor, and a room full of nothing but fairy princess-looking carriages—golden, jeweled, and elaborately carved. There were objects more than a thousand years old. Because of our schedule, we saw only a fraction of the treasures, all stunning.

The following day we endured a nine-hour flight to Khabarovsk, and there the adventure really began. Our days were filled with basically four activities: sleeping, singing, eating, and shopping.

Khabarovsk is a city of about half a million people with many older buildings that look faintly Asian in architecture and are painted bright colors. (Remember where it is...) In the center of town is a lovely square plaza with a huge fountain in the middle.

Despite all the beauty, our hotel was drab and Soviet modern, and huge apartment buildings in Khabarovsk were as drab and ugly as in Moscow. Our rehearsal space was in a huge theatre that was bright yellow on the outside, just down the street from a large pink building.

Temperatures in Moscow had been in the thirties. Khabarovsk meanwhile had snow on the ground and temperatures below zero. Luckily, though, I didn't freeze to death–I bundled up with a long, heavy woolen coat, polartec gloves, scarf, and hat, and I was fine, even when out shopping. The buildings were so hot inside that we frequently pulled off our boots and sweaters. In most of the buildings, the government still controlled the heat—an after-effect of communism that survived.

Russian women dressed to the nines. They are very fashion conscious, and most wore spiked heels. They also loved their furs. There were amazing furs everywhere, such as mink, sable, and chinchilla. *PETA* obviously doesn't go near them. There were fur hats, too, and leather coats and boots lined in fur. Since the temperature was at or below freezing all the time, the fur didn't surprise any of us. The furs there also weren't as expensive as in America. (A lot of the guys bought Russian hats, though I think most of them were fake fur.)

Many Russians do not, alas, share the American customs of bathing every day and using antiperspirant. We noticed that orchestra members would often wear the same clothes for days in a row. (The smell of body odor was everywhere, even in the plush hotel in Moscow.) The water in the Khabarovsk hotel was often brown and malodorous, and I thought it might account for some of their aversion to bathing. I frankly didn't want to bathe in it every day, either, but I did.

I also noticed that Russians smoke a lot, and openly. They

apparently don't fear cancer. The smell of cigarettes was everywhere, as were ads for cigarettes, which I hadn't seen in years. (The Marlboro Man is a popular figure.) They also drink a lot of alcohol—we went to a grocery store on the first day and fully half of it was stocked with booze.

Bathroom facilities were always an adventure, too. The minute I got off the plane in Khabarovsk and went to find a ladies' room, I discovered what we came to call "squatty potties." These are similar to holes in the floor, but have plumbing fixtures that actually flush. They require some aiming—I am now much more sympathetic to guys. Some of the nice restaurants had squatties, as well as the public bathroom at the auditorium where we performed the *Messiah*. We learned to take tissue with us everywhere, too, as there was often no toilet paper. (If there was, it was more like a paper towel or butcher paper, anyway.)

Modesty is unknown there. Men's and women's bathrooms aren't always marked. I learned to just lock the door and not care—and count myself lucky if it wasn't a squatty. One of our guys was in the public bathroom at the hotel in Khabarovsk and a cleaning lady came right in without knocking. She proceeded to clean around him as he stood there tinkling and seemed oblivious, he reported.

I practiced my few words of Russian every chance I got: *please, thank you, hello,* etc. Saying hello was a challenge—the word sounds like *zuhdrastvee-cheh* and doesn't exactly roll off the tongue. Some of the older choir members had never used any Russian, but, by the end of the trip, most everybody had mastered *spassiba* (thank you).

The phrase I used most often, I think, was *vodah byez gaza* (water without carbonation). The Russians drink more booze than water, but I was with Baptists. I think the Russians were amazed that we drank only water, tea and coffee. We had to pay extra for bottled water at nearly every meal. Russians typically drink beverages *after* the meal (not during), so they probably thought us weird in drinking while we ate.

We rehearsed the *Messiah* every day with the orchestra and after dinner most nights as a choir only. The orchestra director, Mr. Teitz (pronounced "tits"—no kidding) was a very demanding perfectionist. (In fact, he was often a screaming dictator. I later learned that this is typical Russian behavior for teachers and artists.) He constantly told the tenors and sopranos to sing louder and we had trouble keeping our voices healthy and strong. We were being pushed to the limit.

We also did several programs in schools, as well as some sightseeing. It was fun and stressful at the same time. I wanted to record everything so I kept a trip journal. I assumed that it would be my one and only trip to Russia.

It's always interesting to go back in your memory and realize that the moments which change your life often seem small and insignificant at the time they are happening.

Chapter Two

MEETING ALESIA

It was Friday, January 23, 2003. I was tired from a long day of rehearsing The Messiah. The schedule for the next day included a morning rehearsal followed by a free afternoon and an evening school performance. In the hotel room after dinner, I slept hard.

It was that night that I had an odd but very powerful dream. I was in an orphanage in a dark room. One figure, however, was bathed in light—an adorable little blonde girl. She walked up and looked at me, smiling, and raised her hands silently requesting that I pick her up. Somehow I knew that this child was mine. *I knew her.*

The dream didn't make much sense on Saturday morning when I first awoke, pinned beneath the scratchy wool blanket in the hotel room, listening to the snores of my roommate. It was still very vivid, but I couldn't fathom why I had dreamed it. Though I had always wanted a family, I had never before dreamed, literally, of having a child. I felt God was trying to tell me something, but that thought was rather scary.

At breakfast, we learned our evening concert had been canceled. One of our members, Danny Griffin, a musical missionary from Ohio, made a proposal to the group. Danny travels to Russia frequently and works closely with the children at Topolevo orphanage. He asked if we would be willing to go to the orphanage that night and sing for the children since our evening was unexpectedly free. All twenty of us agreed. Startled by the change of plans, especially the part about the orphanage, I couldn't stop thinking about the face of the child in my dream.

The rest of the day was spent rehearsing and then shopping. The *Messiah* concert was the next day, so we bought gifts for all the orchestra members (in Russia, gift-giving is very important) and souvenirs for ourselves. The day seemed to drag by as we walked the streets. I wanted to get to the orphanage.

Danny arranged for us to go late that afternoon. As the sun was setting, we piled on the bus and set off. With us was Svitlana, a young woman who works as a missionary ministering to orphanages in the area, helping out with things they need. She lives in Khabarovsk and Danny's church helped her financially.

We prepared for the excursion by gathering (at Danny's request) all extra toiletries and supplies that we could to donate to the orphanage. I ransacked my room and contributed my stash of granola bars, extra hand cream, bandaids, most of my bottle of multivitamins, my extra polartec gloves and scarf, and an extra set of long underwear. Some people threw in extra sweaters and other items such as tampons. We stopped in town so that Danny and Svitlana could buy additional supplies.

The orphanage was not at all what I expected. It was a large, kind of ramshackle building, very dark and forbidding. As the bus came to a stop, a little figure flew across the snow and waited for the bus doors to open. As they did, I stared down into the face of the child in my dream. An angelic-looking little doll with green eyes and short blonde, curly hair, she was wearing a grey and white striped sweater that was too big–but no coat despite the fact that the temperature was in the twenties. As I looked into her face in utter shock, I thought, *I know you!* But, of course, my rational mind said, *That's crazy.*

When I got off the bus I had to use the bathroom, as usual, and I asked Danny where it was located. Danny asked the tiny girl, in Russian, to show me to the bathroom. She took my hand

and led me inside. We went inside and she led me down a dark hallway, then went up to a grownup in an office and loudly and authoritatively asked for the key to a bathroom. She argued vehemently and I smiled to myself. *She has a lot of spirit!* I thought. She then showed me to a locked bathroom with–joy of joys– a European potty. It was quite clean by Russian standards. She made a big effort for me and I was touched. When I was through and came out, I gave her a piece of gum. I regretted that I didn't have anything else in my purse I thought she would like.

This girl led me upstairs to a large room where there were a number of children and the rest of the choir members. I put my backpack and coat on a sofa and took out my camera. She immediately wanted me to take her photo with Tim, another choir member, and then Tim took a photo of her with me.

I was surprised to see that all the kids were older, somewhere between ages seven and seventeen–no babies or toddlers. I was actually relieved because I thought it would be hard to see neglected babies in cribs—like a news story I had heard about Romanian orphans. These children were dressed in shabby clothes and were thin, but none seemed to be in obvious distress.

We sang some songs for the kids while Tim played the guitar. It was "praise music." We had been given lyric sheets before we left Atlanta, but I was not familiar with any of it. There were other songs, too, which I didn't know, but I hummed along or "watermeloned" (mouthed the word *watermelon* as if I knew the words).

The children also sang a couple of songs for us, accompanied by Svitlana. It was strange, the kids sitting at one end of this room in chairs and on the floor and our standing in a group in front of them, many of us snapping photos left and right. Svitlana played a small keyboard when the kids sang.

When the singing was over, Danny said to the kids in Russian that it was okay to come and hug us, and they did. The little blonde girl found me, grabbed me in a tight hug, and wouldn't let go. I held her thin little body close and hated to leave her. Tears started to form and I didn't want to cry in front of the child, so I gently pulled her arms away and asked another choir member, Shirley, to hold her so I could get my coat. I grabbed my things and hurried downstairs to the bus.

Needless to say, every member of the choir was affected by our visit to the orphanage. One of the men got on the bus and said quietly, "Well, that just tears you up."

I sat there on the bus with my face to the window and cried quietly. My heart ached for all those children who were older, who stood almost no chance of ever being adopted. I wanted to take them all home, particularly the little blonde girl. I closed my eyes but their faces were still there.

Suddenly, the thought that I could adopt the little blonde girl popped into my head, but just as suddenly, it seemed like an overwhelming task. I couldn't imagine how to start. Even so, I couldn't help feeling that I was leaving a family member behind.

Chapter Three

LOOKING AT ADOPTION

When I got home I was hit with the news that my company was preparing for reorganization and that there would be job layoffs. My job status was uncertain. I was preoccupied for several months with thoughts that I might soon be unemployed.

A number of people in the legal department quit. I liked my job there and I liked Madeline, my boss. So I wanted to wait, see what happened, and not just quit like so many others. I hated the thought of going back to the drudgery of a law firm. I had been a paralegal in several law firms where I made very little money and had to do a lot of demeaning work for little pay. The corporate lawyers were more easygoing and I made decent money.

However much I feared the layoffs, I couldn't get the little blonde girl out of my mind. When I thought of how she had clutched at me before I left the orphanage, it just tore at my heart and I wanted to cry. I thought about how lost I had felt when I was little and my mother was in the hospital. I hadn't been able to see her or hug her for days on end and had been devastated, despite my father and grandparents being there to comfort me. I couldn't imagine growing up in an orphanage.

I thought, God, I know I can't do much but maybe I could somehow help that little girl—even if I can't adopt her. I tried to put her out of my mind and turn my attention to other things. That didn't last very long.

On February 5, about a week after we got home, I sent an e-mail to Danny Griffin asking if he could help me figure out the identity of the little blonde girl. I forwarded the photo of the little girl and me. He replied:

Sure I remember you.

You will find the photo of Alesia on page two of "Meet the Children." (He inserted a Hyperlink). *Contact California Adoption Center and they can help you adopt this child. I met with the director of the orphanage and he said that he would be happy for anyone to adopt a child from his orphanage.*

I eagerly clicked on the website and held my breath. I scanned the faces and found the tiny photo of her. It was clearly the same child. There she was! *She is so pretty*, I thought. The website contained Alesia's explanation of herself, as follows:

My name is Alesia Pavlova. I am 11 years old. I do not have a father, grandfather, brothers or sisters. I only have a mother and grandmother, and I live without them. When I grow up, I dream of becoming a doctor. I repented on May 16. Now I want to know more about God. I like to study the Bible and learn Bible verses by memory. I recognized that God loves me and that is my biggest revelation.

I stared closely at the little photo. I was stunned at her age. She was eleven years old! I had guessed that she was about eight. She was so tiny! The thought of adopting a child of eleven was really scary.

I sat back in my chair, trying to absorb the news that she was so much older than she looked. I closed the website. I left my cubicle and got some water. I walked around the office. I thought about it. Lunch hour ended. I tried to work, but it was impossible. I couldn't stop seeing her face and thinking of her in that orphanage.

In less than an hour, I decided that the thought of leaving her in that dismal place with no help far outweighed any apprehension about potential issues with an older child. I decided to trust God in the matter. I felt he had put me there in Russia, in that orphanage, for a reason—to find Alesia. How could I adopt her, though?

My mind kept flip-flopping on the adoption idea. Adopting Alesia seemed impossible but surely I could help her. Danny recommended an agency in California that handled a lot of adoptions of children in the Russian Far East. I sent an e-mail to the California Adoption Center the same day, telling myself I was just looking into it. I got this back from their coordinator, Masha Baum:

Hello Dee: I hope you enjoyed your trip to Khabarovsk. Thanks for your e-mail inquire and plans to work with our agency. Certainly I will check on a girl you mentioned and let you know if she is available for adoption.

I was somewhat startled to see that Masha had assumed I wanted to go forward with an adoption. I kept thinking about it, then saying to myself, *No way! I can't afford it. It can't happen! Just do whatever is possible to help!* I could only admit to myself that I was really investigating adoption. Actually adopting her still seemed only a remote possibility for a lot of reasons, but mainly because of my fears of what might happen with my job.

The word "adoption" was becoming more familiar to me, however. I waited a few days and then sent an e-mail to Svitlana, the missionary. I was aware that she knew some English. I got back the following on February 14:

Dear Dee,

It was pleasant for me to get acquainted with many of group of chorus "Messiah". For me and for children—orphans there were many bright memoirs.

I want to help you with your desire. I know, that you pray for it. For the beginning, please, write a little about itself if want. Also write, please, the letter for Alesia Pavlova. I shall translate it and I shall pass her. I shall speak with director about how it is possible to make correctly all steps, and you pray for me, please.

My next e-mail from Svitlana the next day was also in stilted English, but the meaning was plain:

Hi, dear Dee, next week I can find out more information on, whether there can be Alesia your daughter.

Tomorrow I shall see her at a lesson and I shall   simply pass greetings. I think, that it will be pleasant for her. As always the attention is necessary to each child simply.

The word "daughter" struck me. I hadn't really considered all the ramifications of suddenly having a "daughter." That gave me pause. I didn't want her to tell Alesia hello from me. I didn't want to even let Alesia be reminded of our painful parting unless I was sure she was adoptable.

According to the adoption agency's website, only ten percent of children in Russian orphanages are adoptable. I thought it was cruel to get Alesia's hopes up if I couldn't ever adopt her. With the best of intentions, though, Svitlana went ahead anyway. On March 3, I got the following e-mail from Masha at the agency:

Hello Dee:

I just received not great information concerning Olesya. Our agency Khabarovsk representative called to the Topolevo orphanage trying to talk about Olesya and her possible adoption. The gentlemen who is the Director of the orphanage refused even to discuss this subject as he is against the whole idea. Our agency works in other orphanages of Khabarovsk, so if you would like to adopt a younger child from the different orphanage, we can discuss it.

I sat there and read it three times. I was startled. I forgot about my fears of adopting Alesia. This was terrible. I was angry. Who *was* this director anyway? How could he deny this child a loving home? I sent Masha another e-mail:

Thank you so much for your help. I am surprised that he would not discuss it. Does he object to me since I am not married? Perhaps he does not want her to come to America? How strange. As soon as I know my job situation I will get back in touch with you about an adoption.

Masha's reply didn't help:

Director of the orphanage's objections based not on you person-ally, but in concept of adoptions of children by foreigners in general.

I tried to busy myself with my life and forget about the adoption idea. I thought that perhaps this was a sign that it was NOT meant to be. My dream was just a fantasy. I was living a delusion.

And then on March 5, another blow occurred. In reply to an e-mail where I had asked if their representative could perhaps persuade the director to change his mind, Masha replied:

I don't know if our agency is capable to work with the

*orphanage which director is so hostile to the whole idea of adoptions
and practically hang up the phone on our representative. I'm also
sure that she started conversation telling him about you and your
inquire as I passed it to her. I afraid that your missionaries are getting
impressions that they are welcome because of all their support and
help they give to the orphanage and we get real attitude because we
are the local ones to who real attitude could be demonstrated.
Without orphanage cooperation adoption is not possible.*

   *If upon Danny's next visit to the orphanage anything will truly
change, we can work somehow, if not, we only can propose to you an
adoption in other orphanages we work successfully of the younger
girl. Still we even don't know if Olesya is even legally adoptable as
Director of the orphanage didn't want even discuss this subject.*

I sat back and thought, my brain churning in anger. How
could I get through to this obstinate orphanage director? I knew
Svitlana was an ally as a missionary who worked with all the
orphanages in the area, but I didn't think she could help.
However, Svitlana went to work on my behalf. She sent this the
same day:

   *Dear Dee, in this letter I will write you of how the
director of the orphanage sees the adoption. Maybe you could get
upset, but there's still hope. I talked with him more about the adoption
of Olesia. And he resists giving his agreement to adopt Olesia.
However, he doesn't resist of any kind of help. This could be clothes,
medicine, education, writing via mail, etc. He believes that it is more
important to make any help for children in the country where
children are from and only when they get older, they should decide
themselves where and with whom to live.*

   Observing all these things, I again want to offer you to continue praying of Olesia and to keep touch with her, to help her if it is possible, to let her feel your support in the case if God clearly told you that she could be your daughter. But this step is a step of faith, because if you really think of Olesia, than you must not loose hope, but to begin with the things that are able now. If you don't mind, I would like also to know why your choice is on Olesia. If to adopt any other child, I could try and help you talking in other orphanages which are plenty and I am sure you will not be denied there. This is not my direct ministry of adoption, I really want to bring Good News to children, help them how I can. But according to adoption, I will try to do what I can.

With love in Christ, Svitlana.

Although a short time earlier I had been very hesitant to start the adoption, now the orphanage director's attitude infuriated and galvanized me. I was touched by Svitlana's letter, though. She worked with these kids all the time. I sent Svitlana this e-mail in reply:

I am disappointed that the orphanage director won't let the children come to America. I suppose people in Russia are not too happy with Americans right now because of the impending war with Iraq. I cannot explain why I felt such a connection to Alesia, but I did. When I got off the bus, she was waiting, and she showed me to the bathroom. I just felt like she needed me, and I should ask about adopting her, and perhaps I was meant to do that.

(I didn't want to share with her that I had dreamed of Alesia because I was afraid she might think I was crazy).

I pray for Alesia and for all the children.

I don't know what to do about sending assistance. Several weeks ago, I sent Danny Griffin's church a check to be sent to the orphans, and I don't know if that has gotten to you yet. It was for $150 American. I would like to send Alesia whatever she needs that I can afford (clothes, music, books, school supplies?), but I don't want her to become hopeful I can adopt her if that is never possible. I would not want her to be disappointed. On the other hand, I would like to help her. I will pray about it. Any advice you can give would be appreciated.

I am copying Danny on this so if it's unclear he can explain to you (in Russian) how I feel.

Take care, Dee

Danny replied and told me that no American had ever been able to adopt a child from Topolevo. He and his wife, it seemed, had been trying for some time to adopt a child there, Natasha.

I was stunned. NO child from Topolevo had ever been adopted by an American?! How could that be? Khabarovsk was a large town, the biggest town in the region, and there were Americans traveling there all the time. Several missionary groups were active in the town. I couldn't fathom someone being so cruel that he wouldn't let Alesia be adopted. All I could think was that the director was old-line communist and just thought we were all evil.

On March 12, Svitlana sent me a long and personal e-mail that touched me greatly, despite the awkward phrasing:

Dear Dee,

I want to tell to you a little about myself. Mine the daddy and mum have left in the sky to the God. I do not have parents. Several years ago one old person, the brother in the Christ, started to support me. Now always at the end of winter, spring, summer, autumn, he sends me support. He started it to do in the beginning of my missionary service. He does not ask, that I do, he simply helps me personally. He speaks, it to you personally. I always know, that if I have needs personal, or there is no finance to pay for an apartment, or I need to buy something simply for themselves, or for service, at the end of winter, or spring, I can make it. Because he to worry about me personally, not because I do something, that is why, that I am in family Divine. For me his love and care are very important. I never saw him, he already old and is sick, I pray for his health. I do not know, who will care of me, when also he will leave to the God.

You know, why I write to you it? Because to each child who lives without parents, it is very important, that someone cared of him, someone loved him simply so. Even if it is impossible to see this person, it is possible to know, that there is someone who will not leave. If you will send something for Olesia, I can transfer her it, or buy. There will be together with her to shop ... she is very happy because, that someone far remembers her. If you will write to her letters, I shall pass them.

Thanks that has written to me why you want to support Olesia. When I the first time have come to this orphaned house, the girl has approached to me, her name is Snezhana, she is very close to me. I too cannot adopt her. I do not have husband and there is no apartment. Moreover, I the teacher, I cannot allocate someone. But I try to make something for her, very imperceptibly, but personally. It is difficult, but it something.

I send you the address for the orphanage director:
Do not lose hope. The god will help you.
With love in Christ,
Svitlana.

I knew it must have taken a great effort for Svitlana to write the letter and translate it. She was an orphan too—no wonder she could relate to the children in the orphanages.

I felt that she was trying so hard to connect Alesia with me, because she knew I could probably find a way to adopt her, as she could not adopt Snezhana. What a sad situation for her.

I wanted to stay in touch with Svitlana and reach out to Alesia. Svitlana asked me for a photo to give Alesia. She agreed to translate any notes I wanted to e-mail and give them to Alesia. I e-mailed her a scan of the photo that I had taken in January with my arm around Alesia's shoulders and sent her a note to give to Alesia.

I painstakingly put the note into Russian, after finding a website that would translate it. I later realized this is how my note got translated into Russian:

March 12, 2003

Regards, Alesia. Me call Dee Thompson. I visited you during January when I it sang from the mansions of the Messiah. I do not know if you remember me, but I can send photograph to you. I am assistant to attorney with Garland Hotels. I remember your beautiful eyes and your large smile. I took pleasure to attend Khabarovsk and meeting much charming Russian people, including you. I was also happy sing the Messiah.

The Messiah reports the story of Christ. I not entered the marriage and I do not have any children. I would want to write you and to understand you. My dear color dark-blue [my favorite color is blue], and I love the autumn, when sheets change color [I said in English, leaves]. I also love chocolate, cinema, and singing. What things you do love to make

Your friend, Dee

A couple of weeks passed. I didn't hear anything back from Svitlana. I was very stressed out, still wondering if I would get laid off.

I had to know more about the situation with Alesia, however. The thought of adopting her was becoming more and more a possibility and, frankly, one happy thought in the midst of so much chaos.

Not only were things tense at work, but the situation with my boyfriend Sam was tense. He spent more and more time at church and less and less time with me. I liked him and I missed his calls and our dates, which were becoming more infrequent.

I had known when we started dating that he didn't want children, but I kept thinking I could change his mind. I had also known he had a lot of suspicion about my being "saved." I am Episcopalian and he's not—but we believed in the same God, so I couldn't see how it could be a problem. I knew I loved him, but love never lets you see your beloved in a logical, objective manner.

On March 25, I sent Svitlana the following:

Hi there—did you get a chance to give Alesia the letter from me? What was her reaction?

I hope to find out next week whether or not I will lose my job. That will help me know what I can do about an adoption.

I am praying for you and all the children you help, and the continued success of your ministry.

Go in peace to love and serve the Lord.

Dee

Chapter Four

THE DIALOGUE BEGINS

On April 4, I turned on my e-mail and scanned the messages. With great excitement, I saw that I had received my first message from Alesia, translated by Svitlana. It was like hearing her voice, at last, in my language. Despite the awkward English, I was thrilled. I must have read and re-read it ten times:

> *Greetings dear Dee,*
> *I wanted to receive your photo; Svitlana has given me of it, thanks!*
> *I love summer because it is hot in the summer and it is possible to float in the river. Still to me to like somewhere to go.*
>
> *My favorite color pink and yellow. I am glad, that you have written me the letter and have sent a photo. I love dogs. I like to read, draw and play different games. I very much liked how you sang in chorus. That's all.*
> *I Love you.*
> *Alesia.*

I read the letter and thought, except for the awkward translation, she sounds just like an American little girl. I was very heartened. She didn't sound like a traumatized orphan who couldn't express her feelings.

I sat at the computer, closed my eyes, and pictured Alesia in my mind. She was a little girl wearing a yellow shirt and pink shorts, playing with a puppy. She was surrounded by light.

She was laughing.

Tiny seeds of real hope appeared in my heart.

My job situation was dire. I was told at the end of March that I was being laid off and that my last day would be April 11. I frantically started sending out resumes, trying to find any job I could get. I really didn't want to go back to a law firm, but I had to consider everything.

For a paralegal, a job working in-house for a large company's legal department is usually less stressful because time doesn't have to be billed. In a law firm, time is billed out all day long—every memo, call, letter, etc. has to be written down and described perfectly so the client will pay for the task and understand why it's important to the case. Many clients won't pay for certain tasks they consider clerical, and most lawyers don't hesitate to ask paralegals to do clerical work if the secretary isn't handy. Unless you get lucky and work for a kind and decent lawyer, working as a litigation paralegal in a law firm is very stressful. I hated the thought of going back.

My panic was short-lived, thankfully. A couple of days before my last day, I was called down to human resources and was told another paralegal was quitting, so I could keep my job. Relief washed over me.

I knew the paralegal who was leaving. She handled a lot of contracts. They asked me if I could learn contracts and I said, "Sure, I just need some training." I knew nothing about contracts, but anything seemed preferable to being out of work or back at a firm.

I was pleased to not be laid off, but still insecure about the company. Nobody knew what would happen. We were in the midst of an attempted hostile takeover. I read the Wall Street

Journal to try and determine whether or not the new owner would fire everyone if the takeover was successful. Eventually, however, the takeover failed.

It was quite a while before the job felt secure, however. The company canceled all raises and cut out extras, like the service that watered the plants and the service that made coffee.

On April 13, I got another note from Alesia. It was a bright spot in an otherwise bleak time:

> *Dear Dee, I very much would want to receive from you letters.*
> *Today at us the holiday—birthday 12 children was. Svitlana has prepared them for gifts, and for all of us tables have been beautifully covered, there were sweets, oranges and different drinks. It always a good holiday.*
> *On Monday I do lessons, and I have time to take a walk in a court yard. I study 5 days: Monday, Tuesday, Wednesday, Thursday and Friday, and on Saturday and Sunday at me the day off. Earlier we studied and on Saturday, it was difficult for me. Now, well, I have two days off.*
> *When at you birthday? At me on July, 9. I study in 5 class.*
> *That's all. Write, very much I wait the letter from you.*
> *I love you, Alesia.*

Although it shouldn't have made any difference, the fact that our birthdays are close together (mine is July 4) pleased me. I felt a stronger connection to her. I could understand the temperament of someone who is a Cancer.

The next Saturday, I went to Walmart and bought Alesia several gifts. After pondering everything for a long time, I bought her a set of colored pencils, some notebook paper, and a stuffed animal—a dog. I got her some moisturizer, and a new toothbrush and toothpaste. I picked out two shirts for her, one pink and one yellow. I could only guess at the sizes. I also put in a bag of candy for all the kids to share. I just hoped that, if the shirts didn't fit her, they might fit one of the other children. I mailed off the package to Svitlana with some anxiety as to whether or not Alesia would like what I had picked up, but great optimism that it would give her joy to know I was thinking about her.

I kept hoping I would hear that Svitlana had gotten the package for Alesia. I finally e-mailed her, and got this reply on April 20:

> *Dear Dee,*
>
> *I yet did not receive a package from you for Alesia. I did not receive anything, it is a pity. To Russia sending from America go more months. As soon as I shall receive, I at once shall give all to Alesia.*
>
> *Today I have given your letter to Alesia, she was very glad, but the answer yet has not written. She sent the regards to you and the love.*
>
> *Thanks for pleasure which you bring during Alesia's life.*
> *With love, Svitlana.*

On May 4, I got the next e-mail from Svitlana. The package had not arrived. I was rapidly giving up hope that my package would ever reach her. However, my heart leaped when I saw that Svitlana had included another note from Alesia!

> *Greetings, Dee,*
>
> *Excuse, that I for a long time did not write to you. I studied a lot of time. To me to like to receive from you letters. Write to me, please. I very much thank you for your good letters, for kind words,*

*that you write. We have very well noted Easter. Light has brought
sweets and drinks. The good holiday was!!! It is a pity, that you could
not see it. And how your Easter has passed?*
   I love you, Alesia.

On May 31, Svitlana e-mailed to say the package for Alesia
was still not there. I was irritated, and wished I had sent it regular
mail instead of overnight.

*Dear Dee, Unfortunately I yet have not received a sending for
Alesia. A sending yet in Khabarovsk. Obviously, it on customs house
in Moscow. Usually the sending from America comes in 2 months
after sending. I think that already I can soon receive all. Do not
worry.*
   *Alesia goes on Sunday school constantly, she has successes. She
very much values your letters, she is simply happy, when receives
letters from you. Thank you.*

I knew Svitlana was trying to comfort me by telling me
Alesia was happy with just letters, but I had tried to do more.
Perhaps this was a bad sign. Perhaps the logistics of this were too
much.
   On June 2, another note came from Alesia. It brightened me
up a lot. I was also pleased to hear again that she liked dogs
because I love them, too.

*Greetings, Dee, How at you an affair? At me all is normal. And
at you? We went in city but not every day. On June 1 to us there has
arrived Svitlana with a team and they have brought trampoline, we
on it jumped and was cheerful. I every day walk. At us dogs live in a
court yard, them call: the Nolla, Greta and Loza. I do not study in*

the summer and all children in Russia on a vacation all the summer long. On June, 16 girls go in sports camp "Constellation". I probably too shall go in camp, but for the present have not decided I shall go whether or not.

   Well all right, up to a meeting. Write to me, please.
   With love, Olesia.

I was so frustrated with the situation regarding the package. Finally, on July 1, I got the e-mail I had been waiting for:

Greetings, Dee, At last I have received a parcel for Alesia. There is everything that you have sent, according to the list. In some days I shall be in Topolevo and I shall transfer all Alesia. This good business for me, I know, that there will be a lot of pleasure at Alesia, at it soon birthday!!! Thanks you for love to children and thank God for all!

   I WISH YOU Happy birthday, on July, 4, I remember and with day of independence of America!

I remembered that Alesia's birthday was on July 9, and I thought well, perhaps God wanted her to have the package closer to her birthday, and that's why it was held up. I just wished Svitlana would go ahead and give it to her.

Despite my fear that the orphanage director wouldn't let me adopt Alesia, I wanted to know more about Russian adoption. I sent some questions to Masha, the agency representative.

Masha's attitude (obvious from another e-mail) was that I should just adopt a different child, not Alesia, but I just couldn't bear to seriously consider it. My heart said Alesia was meant to be my child and nobody else. I also thought that if I wrote a letter to the orphanage director myself explaining how wonderful it would be for Alesia in America, he might change his mind. I was cautiously optimistic.

On July 20, I finally heard from Svitlana again. She included a note from Alesia. She had gotten the package! Hallelujah. I couldn't tell from the note, but I hoped Alesia had gotten the package sometime around her birthday:

> *Dear Dee, Forgive me, that could not write to you at once about that, I already for a long time have given a parcel to Alesia, at once, as have received, she this very day has written you the answer. Its letter:*
>
> *Greetings Dee,*
>
> *Today at me remarkable day was. Our tutor and 15 children from an orphaned house went to bathe on city ponds. When we came back in the orphaned house, we have met Svitlana near to its house. She has told to me joyful news that there has come from you a parcel. She has invited me and my girlfriends on a visit and has given me a parcel, has treated us with a strawberry and sweets. Now I write to you the letter at Svitlana houses, I have dressed a yellow jacket which you have sent me. It is very glad to all things which you have sent. Thanks for your love and care.*
>
> *I pray for you and I love you. Alesia.*

I read and re-read the note several times. It had been several months since I had bought the items. I could barely remember what the yellow shirt looked like. I was pretty sure it was a shirt and not a jacket—probably just a translation anomaly. I assumed that since she hadn't mentioned the pink shirt, it had not fit or something. It didn't really matter. She knew I cared—I was thrilled that she knew that. I prayed even more fervently that somehow a miracle would happen and I could figure out how to adopt her.

The biggest obstacle standing between me and the adoption of Alesia was the lack of cooperation from the orphanage. I decided it was time for a letter to the orphanage director.

Chapter Five

HELP APPEARS

In late summer 2003, I knew that Svitlana was having a busy summer running Christian camps for the children. It became impossible to get timely responses to my e-mails. I tried e-mailing her several times. I understood her busy schedule, but I was frustrated since she was my only means of communication with Alesia.

I kept hoping and praying I could figure out how to make the adoption a reality, despite the setbacks. I kept pondering a letter to the orphanage director, and how to get it translated into Russian. But that wasn't the only problem. The orphanage director was throwing up roadblocks, but I wasn't sure how on earth to even finance the adoption.

In mid-July I spoke to a good friend of mine, Margaret Dolan, and told her of my wish to adopt Alesia and my worry about how I could ever pay for it. Margaret and her husband had been trying to adopt a baby for a while, and we traded stories. I had pondered many options—borrowing the money, taking it out of my 401-K, even perhaps waiting until I could sell a screenplay. (I was writing screenplays in my spare time.) I even thought about a second job. No option seemed really promising.

Margaret is a straightforward person and I finally got the courage to ask her how she was financing their adoption. She said she and her husband had refinanced their house and opened up a home equity line of credit to cover the expenses. I immediately realized that my condo, which had increased dramatically in value since I bought it, was a way to make the adoption expenses affordable. When that door opened, I began to think that it might really be possible to adopt Alesia, if I could get the director on my side. I started asking around about mortgage companies I could use.

In early August I found a website for the Russian emigrant community in Atlanta and posted a notice to find someone to formally translate a letter for me. I knew about translation services—I used them as part of my job as a paralegal—but I also knew that they cost a fortune.

I was very blessed to quickly receive a reply. Kate Humphrey became my translator and friend. Kate, a native Russian woman, is married to an American and has two children. Living only about 45 minutes away from me, in Acworth, Georgia, Kate has a college degree in English. I could immediately tell from her e-mails that her command of the language was excellent. Another nice bonus—and strange coincidence— was that Khabarovsk was her *hometown.*

We spoke on the phone, and she agreed to translate the letter to the director of the orphanage. I explained that I had a great opportunity to have the letter put directly into the director's hands, as I had learned that Danny Griffin was going over on a mission trip in August.

Here is the letter I wrote to the orphanage director, dated August 2:

Dear Sir,

My name is Dee Thompson and I live in Atlanta, Georgia, United States of America. I was a member of the choir that sang with the Khabarovsk Symphony in January. Our group visited your orphanage on January 24, and met many of the children.

One child was particularly friendly to me, and her name is Alesia Pavlova. I enclose a photo of her with me. The night before I

went to the orphanage, I dreamed I would meet a little blonde girl
and she would become my child. Seeing Alesia startled me, because
she was the little girl in my dream. [I had asked Kate, who told me
that Russians would probably not think me crazy for having a
prophetic dream.]

I want very much to adopt Alesia.

I am not married and I have no children. However, I have a
large and loving family, and many friends. Everyone would welcome
Alesia as part of my life, and she would be my daughter in every way
except biologically. I would make sure Alesia is loved, educated, and
treated as the wonderful and special child she is. I would make sure
she was well educated.

I understand that you are reluctant to let the children be
adopted and come to live in America. There are many Russian
emigrants living here in Atlanta, and they have an active community.
I know several Russian emigrants. I would make sure Alesia didn't
forget her people, or her homeland. If she wanted to return to Russia
to live as an adult, I would help her in any way possible.

If there is a loving home for Alesia in Russia, of course she
should be there. But if that's not the case, please consider letting me
adopt her.

I figured the letter would at least make it clear that I wanted
to adopt Alesia and that I was aware of his concerns. I tried to
sound dignified, despite the fact that I really felt desperate. After
she finished the translation, Kate e-mailed and asked if she could
write to the director herself. I was touched that she would offer to
do that.

This is what Kate said:

My name is Ekaterina Humphrey. I was born in Khabarovsk. I live in Atlanta now near where Dee lives, whose letters I translated for you and Alesia.

Let me use this opportunity and tell you about the life of the Russian community in Atlanta. There are over 50,000 of us here (And this is just in Atlanta. There is a large Russian community in almost every big city in the USA). Many work here, some followed their parents, some followed their children, some got married, some came to study here and some came as religious refugees. All of us are from different towns in Russia and the former USSR but America brought us close together and made us friends because we all have the same peculiarity. We speak Russian.

Our children speak Russian even if there are born in the US. We try to teach them Russian, cultivate Russian culture, and teach them to read Russian. Many Russian people have Russian television at home. We have several newspapers published in Russian. There is a Russian kindergarten, Russian teachers. We always hold meetings of Russian speaking people. We cook Russian. We sing Russian songs. Read Russian books.

Russians are respected in Atlanta as they are everywhere in the USA, for their intelligence and education. In 7 years here I have never been demeaned for being Russian. Vice versa, people treat me with special attention because I am from Russia. Many ask me about Russia. They want to know what kinds of people live in Russia? Compassionate, respectful to elders, caring to children? They are interested in common human traits of character.

I want to assure you that very kind, hardworking, tender-hearted people ready to help even if they don't know you live in America, the same as in Russia. Due to my profession (I am a translator), I meet many adoptive parents who adopted Russian children. Many adoptive parents want to continue our acquaintance because it is important to them to preserve the Russian heritage of their adopted children.

*American adoptive parents that I know treat their Russian
adopted children very well. They give them all that parents can
give—love, care and affection plus wealth, prosperity and a future.*

*Times are hard for Russia. Not many people can afford to
adopt children. Children need to have a family very much. There are
so many children in Russian orphanages. Many never will have the
chance that Alesia has.*

*If you have doubts about America and this is the only obstacle
prohibiting you from allowing Dee to adopt Alesia, let me answer
your questions about America. I have many Russian friends in
America. We are all ready to share our opinions on America and
Americans. They are not avaricious capitalists as they are portrayed.
They are simple people just like us. They want to have children,
family, love and kindness.*

With respect,
Ekaterina Humphrey

I cried when I read Kate's letter. I prayed that, even if my
letter had no effect on the orphanage director, Kate's letter might.
The fact that Kate is from Khabarovsk will surely help, I thought.

I also wrote a long letter to Alesia for Danny to take to her.
It felt so nice to write freely, knowing that Kate would not have
difficulty translating my feelings and words.

Dearest Alesia,

*I hope you are having a great summer, and you are getting a lot
of time outdoors to enjoy the sunshine.*

*We are having a cool and rainy summer. I have to take an
umbrella with me everywhere. It's good though, to get the rain. Last
summer we had a drought.*

*The winters here are very mild. It almost never snows. We
sometimes get some cold rain, but that's all. Perhaps once or twice a
year the streets will be icy. Then everyone stays home. I have lived
here ten years, and only seen it snow a few times. Everyone goes
home and stays there until the snow melts—usually within a day or
two it all melts away.*

*I recently learned that there are more than 50,000 Russian
immigrants living here in Atlanta. Atlanta is a very big town. It's not
as big as, for instance, Moscow. It does have several million people,
however.*

*I live in a condominium. It's like an apartment, except that I
own it. It has two bedrooms and two bathrooms, a living room, dining
area, and a sunporch where I have my office. It's very comfortable,
and close to the interstate. My job is 15-30 minutes away, depending
on traffic. There is a nice swimming pool and tennis court.*

*You remember me coming to sing at your orphanage in
January? This Saturday I am hosting a luncheon for everyone who
went. Some of the choir members live far away and can't come, but
many live here in Georgia and are making the drive. We all enjoyed
our visit to Russia so much, that we have continued to keep in touch
with each other.*

*I have never forgotten seeing you last January, and what a
precious girl you are. I have written to the director of the orphanage
to ask if he will let me adopt you. I would love for you to come live
with me here in Atlanta and be my daughter, if you would like that.
When you grew up, you could live anywhere you like—here or in
Russia. You could go to college, and perhaps medical school if your
grades were good.*

*English is not so hard to learn as you might think. My friend
Kate who translated this letter speaks both languages, and perhaps if
you came here to live she could teach you English as well. She thinks*

you could be fluent in a year.

As I mentioned, there are many people here in Atlanta who are originally from Russia. They have a very active community. There are other girls here your age who speak Russian, who could be your friends.

If the orphanage director will not allow you to come, or if you do not want to come to America, we can still be friends. I will continue to write to you. Perhaps when you grow up you could come visit me.

Stay well. Study hard. Pray every day, for God watches over you and hears all prayers.

You are always in my heart and in my prayers.

Much love,

Dee

I sealed up the letters in a large manila envelope and included a contribution for Svitlana's ministry, as well as a small silver cross on a chain for Alesia. I told her in a note that it would remind her that God is always with her. It was exciting just to know Alesia would have my letter in her hands soon.

On August 28, I heard from Masha at the agency again:

Our representative in Khabarovsk is working on your inquire, she is trying to find out from Department of education if Alesya is adoptabel and trying to meet with the Director.

I thought I should tell Danny of the rude treatment of the agency's representative by the orphanage director, since he should know the real story. (You may recall that Danny had been told that the director was happy for anyone to adopt the children.)

> Danny-
> Right after I got your last e-mail I notified Masha at California
> Adoption Center. I have been e-mailing her since you first told me
> about her some months ago—she had tried to call the orphanage
> director and he was rude to her. The lady here who translated my
> letters for me, Kate Humphrey, also knows Masha and recommended
> her. Kate is Russian, but married to an American, and she is origi-
> nally from Khabarovsk. She is trying to help me through friends she
> still has in Khabarovsk.

On August 21, after he had returned from Khabarovsk,
Danny sent me the following:

> Yes, he was rude to my people as well... Perhaps this time he
> will be open to adoption. Alisa was very excited about your letter. She
> has no brothers or sisters, which will make the adoption MUCH
> easier.
>   DG

After a lot of thought and prayer, I decided to finally break
off the relationship with Sam. I knew that it would never be what
I wanted it to be. He just didn't love me the way I loved him and
we argued a lot about religion. As I said, I am Episcopalian. He is
much more conservative.

I kept trying to convince him I was right, which was idiotic
since he was so thoroughly convinced that I was wrong. No argu-
ment would change his convictions and even if it had, he had
made it clear that he didn't want children. The futility of our
whole relationship was encapsulated in his belief that God had
not told him I was the right person for him. It's hard to argue with
that.

I was quite sad, though. I had been so convinced that, despite our differences, we were meant to be together. We enjoyed each other's company and it was very hard to give up my dream of a life with him, but I did. Every night when I prayed, I started saying this prayer: "God, please don't make me spend my life alone. Please send a miracle."

Chapter Six

DARKNESS AND LIGHT

After a wet and cool summer (highly unusual for Atlanta), I thought life couldn't get any stranger. I was wrong. On September 8, I heard bad news from Masha:

Hello Dee:

Latest update- Department of Education of Khabarovsk region finally responded on our inquire concerning the Olesya's listing in Federal Bank for orphans, that she is not enlisted in Bank, which means that she is not legally adoptable. My associate still will try to check with the orphanage if Olesya has any potencial to become adoptable.

I walked over to my friend Kim's cubicle, told her about it, and burst into tears. I figured that my quest was over. I would never be able to adopt Alesia. I wrote my cousin (and close friend) Lesleigh:

My adoption agency let me know today that Alesia is not adoptable. I don't know why—they are going to check into it and let me know. There used to be a rule—maybe still is, I don't know—that children who were healthy weren't eligible. Only kids with cleft palates, clubbed feet, etc. were eligible. I don't know if that's still the rule. Maybe it's just the stupid orphanage director blocking it somehow.

I have been in touch with the translator and she is going to translate a letter for me to send Alesia. I will probably wait a few days so I won't be too emotional when I write it.

On Monday, September 29 I got an encouraging e-mail from Danny, a forward of an e-mail to him from Svitlana:

Dear Danny, Thank God, I for you have good news. I spoke with director in Topolevo. It agrees, that Natasha has gone to America in the summer. It is necessary to send it the invitation to summer that I could do particularly something further. Director also agrees to consider a question on crossing Alesya to America. At us good conversation was.

Danny noted that this meant I had a better chance of getting Alesia. So the director would let one of the girls go to America for a visit? He would consider letting me adopt Alesia? Maybe at last the prayers were being answered. After a roller coaster ride, I was so happy—I started to picture Alesia as my little girl.

I had spent the previous weekend grieving for my cousin and friend, Dan Embry, who was dying after a long bout with cancer. His mother had called me on the previous Friday to ask me to write his obituary. I agreed and I wrote the obituary through my tears.

On Saturday, I drove to Gainesville where Dan was being cared for in a nursing home, and spent most of the afternoon with him. I was shocked at his appearance. Despite being wracked with cancer, he looked peaceful. He could speak a little and thanked me for coming to see him.

At one point, he looked at his mother and then over to me and said, "Doesn't Dee look beautiful, Mom? Isn't she just beautiful?" He was always saying sweet things like that. I was so touched.

On Tuesday, September 30, I sent out the following e-mail to my close friends and family:

My cousin and friend Dan Embry died today. He had colon cancer. He was 48 years old. I send this little prayer request not for myself, but for Dan's parents, George and Carolyn, and all of us who loved Dan and miss him already. The only good thing about this is he is not suffering any more. I keep trying to remember that, but then I keep remembering his smile and it breaks my heart.

Dan had been so encouraging of the adoption. He had written me long e-mails telling me I could do it, not to give up. Most of my guy friends were skeptical of my adoption plans. Danny was wholeheartedly supportive. I cried just regretting he would never meet Alesia. Then I thought, maybe I should be thankful he's in heaven now, and can put in a good word for me with the head honcho there...

I went to Dan's funeral with a heavy heart. I could not bear to look at him lying in the coffin. That was not the image I wanted to remember. For months afterwards, I thought of Dan when I heard guitar solos on the radio—he loved guitar. I thought of him when I saw red hair—he had beautiful red hair. I missed him.

Since the breakup with Sam had been amicable, and I didn't want to attend the funeral alone, I asked Sam to go with me, thinking surely he would support me in my grief, especially since he had known Dan. He turned me down. He had other plans—a church function of some sort. I think that's when I really accepted that our relationship was truly and finally over. His coldness in that instance demonstrated to me that he was not the person I wanted to spend my life with.

On October 3, after much prayer, I signed and mailed off the contract to the California Adoption Center. I thought, heart pounding, *Now it is a reality. Now the real adventure begins!* I was in such a tizzy that I almost forgot to make a copy for myself.

I went home and looked around my condo, picturing Alesia there. Like a Cheshire cat or a happy angel, I could see my sweet cousin Dan laughing at me from every mote of sunshine pouring in through the window.

On October 10, I sent a letter to a local agency my friend Margaret had recommended, asking if they would do the home study required as a part of adoption. I felt like I was taking giant steps, scary but exhilarating.

Once the paperwork was started, I finally told my mother about the adoption. I had been reluctant to share the idea with her until I felt sure it might be a reality. I was afraid she would disapprove—for a couple of reasons. One, she and Dad had talked about adopting another child when I was five years old and Mother had to have a hysterectomy. I vividly remember crying because they would not adopt a little brother or sister for me. Two, I was afraid she would just be too anxious about my adopting an older child and not getting the full motherhood experience. The opposite proved true—she agreed with me that an older child, already potty-trained and somewhat self-sufficient, would be a better match for me. I was so relieved that she was supportive. She had no grandchildren. My brother was divorced with no kids.

Alesia sent me her first letter by e-mail through Kate, the translator. Kate's aunt Tamara (in Khabarovsk) had facilitated the communication. The letter, which was scanned in by Tamara, had little drawings all over it. *Alesia obviously draws well*, I thought. *It's a sign of intelligence and creativity.* I forwarded it to Mom and my brother Bruce:

Dee, I am sorry for not writing sooner. I didn't have time. Who is Tamara Shuiskaya? (Kate's aunt who sends her the letters.) *My favorite times of year are Autumn and Summer. I like to be outside. The leaves are very beautiful. They are yellow, orange and sometimes green. What are your favorite animals? My favorite animals are dogs and cats. My favorite bird is a dove. I like birds and animals. They are very beautiful. I like to eat potatoes, hot-dogs and pigs in a blanket. Also I like cakes and chocolate. What do I like to do? I like to draw pictures, read books and watch movies. I will write you sometimes too. I like nature very much and I will send you a drawing of nature.*

A couple of weeks later, I talked to Masha by phone and asked her many questions about the adoption. I was nervous and took notes about the conversation. The adoption still seemed to be an expensive and daunting task, but the reality of it was becoming more exciting.

I thought a lot about how I would appear to Alesia as a mother. Would I be a young, hip mother or a fussy old hag? Neither description seemed appropriate. Then again, I decided the exercise was silly. Alesia would welcome any mother who loved her.

In early November, Danny Griffin e-mailed me four more photos of Alesia, ones that he had taken when he was at Topolevo in August. They were really sharp and clear. She looked older. In a couple of them she looked very grown up, but my favorite was a shot of her wearing a red shirt and the chain of the little silver cross I had sent her. I took the best two photos and sent them to Mom.

Mom replied:

Both photos came through fine but wish they were not so big. Each came out on two sheets when I printed so will have to tape and cut. She is so pretty. Nice teeth. Nice smile.

As I said, I had been very apprehensive about telling mother about the adoption plans, since I wondered if she would worry and think I was nuts, or be disappointed at not getting a younger grandchild. With each communication, she proved that all my fears were unfounded. Mom was delighted with the photo and news and became my biggest supporter.

My brother, however, was a different story. He didn't say it out loud, but I knew he thought the adoption was a bad idea. I just hoped and prayed he would come around. As adults, we had become close friends. He was usually my great supporter and advisor but for some reason, telling him about the adoption changed everything. I could feel a distance and coldness between us, and it saddened me.

I went to the movie one night with my friend Maria. We had both worked for the same law firm for a while and had known each other for several years. Maria was a single mother raising her little boy. Her ex-husband was long gone and paid no child support.

We walked outside after the movie. It was one of those soft nights you find in the south during the fall and spring—clear and warm, the stars easily visible. I told Maria I had signed the contract with the agency and things were really happening on the adoption. Maria looked startled. "Have you really thought this through?" she asked.

I smiled. "Of course. This is what I want. This is *my* child. I just have to get through the red tape and go get her."

Maria's face was stern. "I don't think you really know what you're doing. Raising a child alone is really tough. You are on duty twenty-four hours a day, seven days a week. I know. It's been incredibly hard for me. You need to really think about that before you commit to this idea."

Resolute, I answered, "I know it's not easy being a single parent. I've watched you with your son. I know also that you get lots of help from your parents and friends."

She was still stern. "That's right. No way could I have managed without a network of people to help. Even so, it's INCREDIBLY HARD, Dee. This child may have a lot of issues."

I was taken aback by Maria's vehemence. She is normally a very calm person. "We will deal with the issues. I have family and friends too, you know. I appreciate your concern, but I CAN manage this," I said.

Maria looked doubtful. I knew she was just trying to be a concerned friend, but I was irritated. We talked a few more minutes, hugged goodbye and went our separate ways. After thinking it over, I decided not to let her discourage me.

Thanksgiving brought a wonderful e-mail from Kate. Her aunt had gotten a letter from Alesia, scanned it, and sent it by e-mail to Kate, who had translated it:

Dee,

My favorite time of the year is summer because it is hot and one can go to the beach and swim. We have a holiday like this ? *(Dee, I think she is referring to the Neptune's Day, which is not really a holiday but it is often held for children at the summer camps and health resorts. Kate's note)* *.*

I like to play games. I like to go to the downtown and go to the movie theaters. I like these movies: Coneheads, The Land of Love, the Land of Hope, Dream Shore and Escape. Yes, I watch American movies. I like them very much. I like these cartoons: Cinderella, Sleeping Beauty, Tarzan and Lion King. I will be glad if you adopt me. Very much.

I had always figured Alesia would be glad to be adopted, but it was nice to see it in black and white. I was also happy she liked movies. That would give us something in common.

The fall passed very quickly. I had a lot of Christmas shopping to do for friends and family. I spent a great deal of time organizing a reading of one of my screenplays—polishing the screenplay, getting actors to read, etc.

I spent a lot of time getting to know my new boyfriend. He was the son of my mother's friends, I'll call him Richard Warren. [Not his real name.] I had not wanted to even meet him, but after the umpteenth nagging call from my mother, I sent Richard a short e-mail just to get my mother off my back. As I typed it I was thinking to myself, it's way too soon to start another relationship. I was still trying to get over Sam.

I knew Richard would be a challenge to date, as he lived in New Jersey and our relationship would be a long-distance one. I took comfort from the fact that he was in the Air Force, but was planning to retire soon and move back to the south.

I made it clear to him from the beginning that I was adopting a child. He reassured me that he liked children. Things went well. We e-mailed and called every day and grew very close, very quickly. He loved making music and cooking—two of my favorite activities. We shared similar views. He was kind and funny, and we spent hours talking on the phone. He had never been married or had children, but had been in several serious relationships.

He came to Georgia over the holidays to see his parents, and we spent a lot of time together. I met his parents. He met my mother. He was so sweet and easy to be with. Time flew when we were together. Unlike with Sam, we never argued. I had never known such happiness in any relationship. I felt we were fated to be together.

I tried not to worry if or when Alesia would get her Christmas presents. I had sent them to Kate's aunt in Khabarovsk before Thanksgiving just to be safe, so the box had been sitting in her office since then. I hoped she wouldn't forget to deliver it to the orphanage. One day, I checked my e-mail and was delighted to find the following report from Kate:

> *Dee,*
>
> *It is the 24th of December in Russia and your Christmas present has been delivered to Alesia. She was overjoyed! She couldn't believe that there was so much stuff there for her and she was very excited about everything.*
>
> *She said to my aunt that she wanted to give you a present too. She didn't say what though. My aunt also brought her more envelopes and some paper. My aunt says that Alesia is a nice, sociable girl with an open clear face. She is 12. My aunt found out that Alesia was from a little village called Pobeda (in Russian it means "Victory"). Alesia's father died but her Grandmother and her mother are alive. They still live in Pobeda and drink very much. She has lived in the orphan house for 5 years. Since her mother is still alive, I guess this was the reason why Alesia wasn't in the adoption list.*
>
> *Merry Christmas!*
> *Kate.*

The thought that her mother and grandmother were both alcoholics was sad. I wondered if that was why she had been taken out of the home. Did they abuse her? Did they neglect her? Had their drinking just prevented them from working and supporting her properly? I shuddered to think what she might have been through. I knew I could not find out more until I made a trip to Russia. I knew I would not be allowed to see her file until I formally applied to adopt her.

I had been surfing the internet and learning as much as possible about adoption, particularly international adoption. I had also started looking for books to read. One of the first I found was *The Russian Adoption Handbook,* by Richard McLean, an American lawyer who had adopted several Russian orphans. His guide was thorough—everything from what to pack to how the Russian legal system works. My research indicated that Russians sometimes hide things about children just to get them adopted. This gave me pause, and I had a lot of time to think about the possibility that Alesia might have a learning disability or deformity—things that sometimes might not be obvious just from meeting a child. I didn't have to think long, though. It didn't matter. I would deal with whatever problems there were, with God's help.

Chapter Seven

2004—THE REAL WORK BEGINS

In early January as I was driving home from work, I started flipping the radio stations around, trying to find a good song. The dial landed on a country station. A song came on by Martina McBride, *My Daughter's Eyes*. As I listened to the words, I started crying. The words "my daughter" had never seemed to apply to MY being a mother.

If the orphanage director didn't block it, I was going to really have a daughter. It just struck me. All the emotions I hadn't allowed myself to feel—hope, fear, and love—came flooding through. I pulled over to the mail hut at the condo and sobbed and sobbed. I might soon have a daughter. What an awesome responsibility as well as a joy. Now I had some idea of how my mother felt about me. Suddenly, I understood her a lot better.

A few days later, I was thrilled to see this e-mail from Kate. I immediately forwarded it to Mom and Bruce and my close friends:

> *Dee,*
> *Below is the letter from Alesia to you. Attached are the draw-ings that she made.*
> *Kate.*
> *My dearest and beloved Dee, thank you for sending me these presents for Christmas. All children loved candies and chewing gum. I want to wish you a Merry Christmas. I made a postcard for you. Most of all I liked the Barbie doll. It is very beautiful and you are*

*very beautiful too. Girls and I staged a play. I was a butterfly. I had a
red dress with pink wings and sparkling horns on my head. I wish I
could send you a picture but unfortunately we didn't take pictures.*

*I am getting ready for school today. I am washing and ironing
cloths, putting textbooks in my school bag because school starts again
in a day. I want it to begin already because I want to see my friends.*

Dee, I love you. Good bye.

(The post card had an angel drawn on it and the following
words):

*I wish you happiness and kindness! I wish you to always be
beautiful and never get sick.*

(The other postcard had a Christmas tree drawn on it and it
said):

Merry Christmas

I was delighted with the note. It sounded genuine—not
something written out of forced politeness. And I loved that she
had drawn an angel. I love angels—I collect them, and I believe
in them. My mother taught me that. I emailed her the note.

Mom replied to the letter:

*Well, at first I wanted to cry .... but then I thought how
wonderful it is that she is talking to us! She is so precious! We are
praying! Do you think she knows about Valentines???? I wish so much
that she could know that she has another Grandma who already loves
her. Well, all in good time! Love you so much!—Mom*

I figured it was time to start really learning Russian, even
though the start of my Russian class had been delayed. I went
online and looked at the Russian alphabet and printed it out. It

looked so odd. Some of the letters in Cyrillic are the same as ours—for instance, *O* and *A,* but others are really strange. *B* is pronounced as a *V,* and *r* is pronounced as *g.* I thought, this is going to be confusing. It's also more complex than our alphabet—thirty-four letters instead of twenty-eight, and two sounds, hard and soft, which are shown with a symbol.

I also bought a set of CD's called *Learn Russian in Your Car.* I started listening and trying to memorize the words. They sounded much more strange and exotic than anything I had ever heard. I had to listen to each word over and over, repeating and trying to remember them. I had to use memory tricks to try and remember words. For instance, the word for you is *tee*—similar to *tu,* which I had learned in high school French class.

On Thursday, February 5, I had my first visit with Susan, the social worker doing the home study. I went to Borders on my lunch hour to meet her. It was a raw, windy, rainy, and cold day. I was so glad I had put all my adoption documents in labeled folders in a plastic file box.

I liked Susan. Susan was a small, plump woman with dark hair. Toward the end of our meeting, I told her about my adoption journal, and she showed me a book called *I Love You Like Crazycakes,* by Rose Lewis, about a single lady who adopts a Chinese baby. The book had beautiful illustrations. I also picked up another reference book, *The International Adoption Handbook,* as well as a true story written by a woman who adopted a baby boy from Russia, *The Russian Word for Snow.* It was hard for me to go back to the office and not read them.

While Susan and I talked, I realized, to my horror, that there was an INS form that I should have sent but hadn't. I explained to Susan that I thought the home study had to be done first, but she said, "No, for the I-600A, it doesn't." Oops. She also said that

I had to go as soon as possible and get my fingerprints made. I called and found out that the DeKalb Police Department had a satellite office close by my work, so I could do that the following Monday.

Since I am a paralegal who is used to collecting and cataloguing documents, I have prepared complex cases to go to trial. Though the documentation required for the home study and for the Russian dossier didn't really intimidate me that much, I was anxious to get it done.

Sometimes, while reviewing the long lists of documents I needed for my homestudy and my Russian dossier, I would start to panic and worry that the INS or some other government entity would not come through. I would always then hear a little voice in my head say, "Pray about it." I would pray, and immediately the anxiety would subside.

I went to my first Russian class, where there were only three pupils, two other women and me. The teacher looked to be about twenty years old, a slight, blonde Russian girl named Anna. She was very patient. We basically just went over the alphabet and read through Russian words that sound similar to English, like *taxi* and *internet*. It was hard to read the tiny print and the letters for *P* and *D* looked so similar. The books also weren't in yet. Anna (our teacher) copied pages from her book. She also encouraged us to get tapes or CD's and listen to pronunciation.

Two hurdles were jumped—meeting the social worker and learning she was helpful and supportive (not an intimidating figure) and starting to formally learn Russian. I felt that, at last things were really moving—I really was going to make it happen and become a mother. It was scary and exhilarating. Yet, I kept telling myself not to start counting the days until Alesia was home. I was still not confident and was afraid to really hope I would have

Alesia home soon.

The next day, I was in a tizzy. I had a run-in with a young lawyer, Peter, who had been added to our team. At times he was affable, but could also be really cold sometimes. I hoped I could figure out how to work with Peter without getting really angry and losing my temper. I didn't want to quit and have to find another job—at least not until after the adoption. However, Peter clearly didn't want a paralegal. His whole attitude was that I should get out of his way.

A couple of years before, I had quit a job at a law firm because the partner I worked for was like Peter. He didn't know what to do with a paralegal—he either gave me secretarial work or tried to make me do legal research and write documents which should have been handled by a lawyer. One day he had come into my office and screamed at me for five minutes because I had not prepared an Answer correctly. It was an extremely complicated case, and I had never done an answer before. He was often horribly unfair and unreasonable. I quit that job as soon as I could.

Now Peter was acting similarly to that attorney. I was dismayed. I had liked my job until he was hired. I didn't want to work with Peter, but I had no choice. I just hoped I could get Madeline to listen to me when I told her about our communication problems.

Madeline had been a wonderful supervisor, at first. She was only a year older than I and was easy to talk to. I felt I could speak freely to her as I would a friend. I had told her I loved to write, and wished I could do it full-time. She was very supportive about the adoption.

However, after the reorganization of the company, a new

department head had come onboard. He was (still is, I'm sure) a cold, ruthless little martinet, totally lacking in people skills. He made everyone paranoid that they would soon be fired, and Madeline became a changed person. We didn't go to lunch together any more. She was never available when I needed to talk to her. I felt very uneasy, though I did the best job I could do and hoped that would suffice.

That weekend, I went to mother's house in Augusta. I read the book *The Russian Word for Snow*. It was a fascinating story. That couple didn't use an agency. I was so glad I was using one. They spent weeks in Moscow before finally getting their baby.

In my mother's house, I had my room I where I always stayed, though I had never lived in that house. It contained my childhood bed and dresser and many other things. I got down from the top of the closet some of my old books to put in Alesia's room—the Robert Louis Stephenson poetry, *Tales from the Ballet*, and a book on how to teach kids to cook. I added it to the book I bought at Borders and a Russian fairytale book I found, so that Alesia then had a small collection—though no books in Russian, alas.

The paperwork for the adoption continued. When I got home, I managed to download and fill out the INS I-600A form. I hoped I had done it right. I had to send them a $510 check, the form, and a copy of my birth certificate.

A week later in mid-February, I sent off an e-mail to my cousin Tony, who is also a close friend. I included in it the latest news on the adoption:

I am deep into the adoption paperwork now. I had to go get fingerprinted at the Chamblee Police Station yesterday. They run a criminal background check before they can approve a home study—

which is a good thing. I also am having to get a lot of letters—veri-fying employment and insurance, recommendations, etc. It's worth it, though. I am getting excited about becoming a mother. I am going to a weekly class and learning Russian, plus I bought some CD's in my car so I can learn phrases. I can now say perfectly in Russian "I do not understand Russian." Just in case I don't understand what someone's saying to me, you know....?!

A few days later, I learned that the agency had gotten Alesia on the database of adoptable children. All children must be on that database before they can be adopted. I sent the following to Danny Griffin:

The good news is that she is on the database, and should be available sometime in May. Hopefully I will have my homestudy done and be ready to go over there then, for the first trip. I hope I can bring her home this summer. I am excited. The orphanage director let the agency put her on the adoptable list, so I hope he won't block the adoption.

Danny replied:

Leonid, the director, has been much more open to us lately. I have been getting warm responses from him. We have been giving toys, socks, tables & chairs and lots of other things to the orphanage to help them. The swing set we built last summer seemed to open some big doors for us. If he has not blocked the adoption by now, and he has put her on the list, then there is no going back.

It took me some time to emotionally process the huge hurdle that had been jumped—overcoming the reluctance of

Leonid to let Americans adopt the children. That had been a big worry to me. More and more hope was in my heart, more optimism. It felt like the start of an exhilarating ride at the fair, scary and thrilling.

Chapter Eight

MORE PAPERWORK

I spent Valentine's Day weekend with my boyfriend, Richard. It was cold and snowy in New Jersey, but I didn't care. All that mattered was being with him. We cooked together, watched movies, and took drives in the country.

It was so wonderful to feel part of a couple again and hopeful about a future with a partner. I had been through such a difficult breakup with Sam. All those hopes of a life with him had been so painful to let go of. Before Sam, there had been a long period with no relationship, just a lot of dates that led nowhere. I felt that Richard was truly the man intended for me, that we were meant to be together.

Richard didn't tell me he loved me, but I felt it when I was with him, even though we had only known each other a few months. His words, his actions, and his concern for me all demonstrated how much he cared. I knew he had been badly hurt by a couple of prior relationships and was apprehensive about saying the word "love." I could wait.

On February 18, my second meeting with social worker Susan went much more smoothly because I felt I had really made strides towards getting my paperwork done. She also said that the criminal background check (my fingerprint cards to the GBI) should be returned to the local agency soon. She explained, "If someone has no criminal record, it usually doesn't take long at all."

I sent an e-mail to Mom, Bruce, and others about my

excitement.

Susan couldn't advise me about gifts to take to Russia, but I got on the internet and looked on my groups for ideas. Gift-giving is a big part of Russian adoption. Russian orphanage officials expect gifts. I also wanted to take things for the children. Later that day, I received an e-mail from Danny Griffin that suggested some gifts, then:

Alisa will be the first child adopted from Topolevo. It has been seven years of hard work and we are praying that the Dear Lord will allow this to happen. God Bless, Danny

Seeing those words in print gave me a sense of wonder. The first child adopted from the orphanage. Wow. I was making a little history.

Even though I thought about her all the time, I realized one day that I had not written to Alesia in a while. I sent Alesia the following, through Kate:

Dearest Alesia,

Thank you for your wonderful letter, and the beautiful draw-ings. I am so glad that you liked the Barbie doll and the other Christmas gifts, and that you shared the candy and gum with the other children. I was happy to hear that you like dressing up and creating plays. I loved doing those things when I was your age.

It is winter here, but not too cold. Tomorrow the temperature is supposed to be 65 degrees. We haven't had any snow. The only snow I have seen is when I visited a friend of mine in New Jersey—it's far north of here. (I was willing to share a little but I did not plan on telling her about Richard being my boyfriend until she got home.)

I have good news. You are now on the official list of adoptable children in Russia. I am working very hard to finish the documents I need to obtain so that I can adopt you. I have had to gather up many letters and a lot of information, so it has taken some time. I hope that perhaps in May I can come over and see you, and start the adoption process in the Russian courts. I would then come home, and return a few months later to complete the adoption, and bring you back here.

My mother is already excited about seeing you and becoming a grandmother. She has your photo and can't wait to meet you. All my friends and their children want to meet you. You will have many relatives and friends when you get here.

Sweetheart, please try extra hard to learn English. I know it's a difficult language, but the more you know, the easier it will be for you when you come to America. Many words in Russian sound almost exactly the same in English—for instance, the words "taxi", "omelet", "internet", "soup", "comfort", etc.

My friend Kate who translates these letters can help you when you get here, and the school here will help you, but you still need to learn on your own. If I can, I will try to get some tapes, to help you. (Kate—feel free to add any comments here that you think would help.)

I am praying that when the orphanage director and his staff see how wonderful it is for the children at Topolevo to be adopted by Americans, that he will let more children there be adopted. There are many Americans willing to adopt older children, not just babies.

Adopted children here in the USA are treated just like biological children. Most parents do not hide the fact their children are adopted -they celebrate the wonderful gift of having children. They are honest about adoption with their children, family, friends and neighbors. There are many Americans who go to Russia to adopt children. I have a friend who has adopted three Russian children, all of them over the age of 8.

Study hard, pray every day, and remember God is always with
you. I pray for you every day, Sweetie.

   Much Love, Dee

I had been reading in some of my reference books about the Russian attitude towards orphans. It was very sad. One book said there was such prejudice towards orphans that parents wouldn't want their children to marry an orphan. Russians often hide from their adopted children the fact that they are adopted. They will also fake pregnancies and then adopt infants and tell everyone it's their biological baby. Because of the attitude of society, many Russian orphans face prejudice in housing, jobs, and socially when they leave the orphanage. Many turn to crime or prostitution. A large percentage of them commit suicide.

I wanted Alesia to understand that in America things are different. I wanted to state clearly that I would love her just as much as a biological child. I already loved her. I couldn't think about it too much though, or it would make me cry.

The next Saturday, I met my friend Maria at Discover Mills mall. While her son and a friend were at the skate park, we walked around the mall. I bought Richard several items for his birthday the following month. I took great delight in picking out cologne he would like and soft new sheets for his bed.

I missed Richard so much that it was a physical ache, at times. I missed his touch, missed his kisses, even his smell. The daily phone conversations were essential and painful at the same time. The visits were all too brief. Picking out things for him helped.

I couldn't forget about Alesia, though. On a shopping excursion with Maria, I kept looking at all the different merchandise thinking, I wonder how that would look on Alesia. I wonder how that would look in her room. I wonder what she will think of this place. Has she ever been shopping?

Maria and I spent a pleasant time at a pottery painting place next to the skate park in the mall. I got a cute bank shaped like a butterfly and painted it yellow, blue, and pink to go with the colors in Alesia's room. I left it to be fired and picked up later.

The next day I took in my *Messiah* concert poster to be framed. Choosing the least expensive options, I still ended up spending $170. However, I thought it important that Alesia would have something Russian in her room and, if it hadn't been for the concert and my trip, I never would have known Alesia.

After I got home, I sat in Alesia's future room for a while and just looked at everything. I tried to picture Alesia in the room. I tried to think about what else was needed—another bookcase? A desk? Would she want a room that looked like a little girl or a teen?

Planning the look of Alesia's room was such a joy. The colors I put in there were blue and yellow, and they predominated in the Tommy Hilfiger quilt on the bed. I also found her matching bedside tables and put them in there. I hung some cheerful yellow curtains. I moved into the room a small white bookcase that had been in my room. I loved making a cozy nest for her, a place of sanctuary. I had always loved being in my room when I was a child.

One day near the end of February, I woke up to about two inches of snow on the ground—a very rare sight in Atlanta. I waited until sunup, then got bundled up and went outside to take photos of my condo in the snow. Just a few days before, I had been thinking, regretfully, of our lack of snow, since the condo looks so much prettier in the snow. God must have heard me.

In early March, I started making a list of all the photos I wanted to include in the little photo album I was taking to Alesia on the first trip. I had decided I wanted her to have photos of everything to do with her future home—my condo, my friends, family members, even her school, the church, and Kroger. America looks so different from Russia—I wanted her to know what home looked like. I didn't want it to seem so strange and foreign to her when she got here. Taking photos helped pass the waiting time, too. I was impatient for her to be home.

Chapter Nine

COMPLICATIONS

On Sunday, March 13, 2004, I got a distressing e-mail from my brother. I had e-mailed him and tried to explain my feelings about the adoption, in hopes of getting reassurance that I could make him Alesia's designated guardian in my will. He didn't reply. I sent him another e-mail. His response was very negative. I knew he was just afraid for me, but it hurt. Obviously I would have to just show him he was wrong.

The next Tuesday I sent off to Mom and Bruce each a package containing a copy of some of the adoption documents I got from the agency—namely the list of documents needed, timeline, and information about Khabarovsk and travel arrangements. I hoped my brother would read it and realize I was dealing with honest people and would get Alesia. I also sent a copy of the journal I was keeping. I explained that it was a work in progress—but I wanted them both to know more about this journey.

My brother's attitude about the adoption bothered me. I respected his opinion but I just knew in my heart he was wrong. I had to just trust God would bring his heart around to us.

The next Thursday, my social worker Susan came to my home for our final visit. I had taken great care to get Alesia's room ready and clean up the entire condo. I hung the *Messiah* poster, and hung the mirror over the dresser. Susan was very complimentary and said several times how lovely everything looked. I always enjoyed decorating my condo and I had spent a lot of time painting and getting new floors put in. It looked homey, I felt.

We basically spent most of the next hour or so sitting at my dining room table, talking. She asked me a number of basic questions about the condo—floor space, laundry facilities, nearby police and fire stations, etc. Did I have a fire extinguisher? Etc.

When she left, I felt relieved, which surprised me—I had not been really nervous about it, I thought. Then again, it was so nice to feel validated, to know the room was looking ready for a little girl.

Thursday night's Russian class was another story. I had not studied as much as I should have, and the grammar points puzzled me. Verbs aren't that bad, but nouns have eight different "cases" and all require different endings. I didn't really care about studying in that much detail.

I took a deep breath and told the teacher I really just wanted to know basic mommy words and phrases—brush your teeth, go to bed, etc. The next day, she e-mailed me a list some adoptive parents had compiled—all the mommy words! It's called Russian Child Talk. It was fifteen pages long. I was so excited to have it.

I really liked that the first phrase in the Russian Child Talk list was "I love you." The words are there in English, Russian, and spelled out phonetically.

I love you. **Ya** teb-**ya** lou-**blue**

One paragraph in the handout just haunted me:

In a Russian home, the kitchen table is the very center of that home. However, in an orphanage, eating is, unfortunately, not the great family experience of a traditional Russian home. Most children learn to begin drinking from a cup before the reach their first birthday and begin to learn to feed themselves quickly. Order always seems to be kept and children learn that their job is to eat when they are at the table. Napkins are not used and there is no emphasis on pleasantries or manners. So, we will not worry here about the etiquette and will concentrate only on very simple manners surrounding eating.

In my childhood, eating meals together was an important family ritual. Mom made sure that we had a hot breakfast every morning and we sat down to dinner together every night. Dad was big on table manners. Mom always asked us to talk and share our day. I knew I wanted Alesia to find pleasure and comfort in meals, not view them in the Dickensian way described in the handout.

On Friday I had several conversations with Mom about the Easter presents she had bought for Alesia. She sent me a list that included Barbie clothes, stuffed toys, pens and flowered notepaper.

We worked out that Mom could mail the presents to me and Kate would help me send them to Alesia. Mom wrote a great note for Kate to translate and send:

Dear Precious Alesia, How wonderful that you are going to become a member of my family! Dee is my daughter and we have lots of happy times together. Now, soon, you will be with us also and I can hardly wait. You will have a very pretty bedroom at Dee's home and, I think, you will really enjoy it. Both Dee and I are very good cooks so we will cook the foods you like. I am looking forward to taking you shopping for some new clothes when you and Dee come to visit me. You will be my first Grandchild and I am so pleased! Until we meet, take care and God Bless You. With much love, Grandmother Elva

All during the phone conversations and e-mails with Mom about the presents, I kept praying, Lord please let this work, let me get Alesia. I don't want this adoption to fall through and break Mom's heart, too.

I spent the next Saturday on the adoption, mostly on looking up information about the nearest police and fire stations and completing paperwork. At the request of the social worker, I bought a carbon monoxide detector. It was about $42. I hoped it would work. I had never really thought about carbon monoxide before outside of science class.

I made a folder for the adoption box labeled *Police* and *Fire* as a reference and, as I was flipping through all the labeled folders, I came to the one with the recommendation letters from my aunt, uncle, and my friends Ricky and Maria. I wrote them a thank-you, and included this:

There was a time in my life when I thought I would never have a family of my own. What seems so easy for most people was, to me, an un-reachable goal. Some years later, after my father died, I realized I have friends that ARE my family. If it were not for the love and support of my friends, I would not be here. Many times I have just felt like giving up. My friends have sustained me.

Thank you both for being there for me. I thank God every day for all the people who love me, and I pray for you, and ALL my friends. I am a very lucky woman. I have been so blessed.

I spent most of the next Saturday reading a book about adoption. I was determined to educate myself as much as possible.

When I checked my e-mail that same day, I found a letter from Mom:

Hi, Sugar, what a joy to read the first part of your journal! Today has been so special to me because it is the first time I have sent

Alesia a direct present from me. I had such fun collecting the gifts for her Easter present —- I won't say "basket" because a basket would be difficult to mail. My biggest problem was to refrain from sending too much! I kept telling myself to wait until she can go with me to shop so that we buy things to HER taste. Also, we don't know her size. It has been so many years since I have paid much attention to what the young/pre teens are wearing that I now have lots to learn.

When you and your brother were small, I used to think that I was going to be really uncomfortable when you became yucky, tacky, teens. How tremendously mistaken I was! I found that I absolutely adored teens! And I am absolutely going to adore "Miss Alesia " and really plan to give my best effort to spoiling her! As you know, I don't cry easily but I cried when I wrote the tiny short note to include in the package. I also included a photo that showed my white streak in my hair so she will know I really look like a Grandma! Dee, you are the light of my life. Thank you for being the wonderful daughter that you are. I pray you will have as much fun with YOUR daughter that I have had with mine!!!

LOVEYA!

Mom

In mid-March, I took a break from the adoption for about ten days—I was thinking about it a lot, of course, but not really doing anything. I was waiting to get the completed home study from Susan. I had been so frantic in my efforts to get all the letters, the fingerprints, and the forms filled out that would work for both Russia and America that I was mentally exhausted.

I got a letter from Alesia, translated by Kate. I was so delighted, and relieved. Kate had sent it on March 5, but my e-mail was been screwed up and I didn't get it.

Here's what Alesia wrote:

Hi Dee,

I will be very glad when you adopt me. I want you to come in May very much and I want May to come as soon as possible. I will be waiting for you. I can't wait for when I leave for America too. Yes, I will study English. I will try very hard.

I love animals, birds, fish and insects but not all. I like to go for a walk. I especially like dogs and cats. I like to clean.

I love you very much and I pray for you every day.

I love you very much and I want to see you as soon as possible.

With love, Olesia

Kate notes:

In English it says: Dee, I love you! The letter is written on a piece of paper covered with red drawn hearts. Kate

Kate sent the photos and drawings later. One drawing was a female figure with a photo of Alesia's head on it. Another was what looked like a dinosaur. I got a chuckle out of the cute drawings. With every letter she seemed more and more real, and the dream got closer.

Chapter Ten

THE HOMESTUDY IS DONE! YAY!

Completing the home study felt like a major hurdle was jumped. The home study painted me as a reasonable, competent person who could raise a child—important validation. It also was a necessity—no child can be adopted, foreign or domestically, without getting a home study done.

My home study process was much easier than some. I read on one of the internet message boards about one single woman trying to adopt who had been grilled for hours on why she wasn't married. I read other stories about families being subjected to unsympathetic social workers who asked embarrassing questions, wrote up home study reports not acceptable to Russia authorities, etc. Susan, on the other hand, was a supporter, and even let me edit and correct the home study before she submitted it in final.

A few days after I sent it, I heard from Masha that the home study was fine for Russia, and I could go ahead and prepare the rest of my Russian dossier documents. I faxed my passport to her so that she could fill in some of the information. I was so relieved that she approved the homestudy—I had been afraid she would want Susan to change a lot of things. Each region in Russia has its own peculiarities.

Getting used to the reality of the adoption was an ongoing process. I hit levels of realization every time I accomplished any major goal, like getting the room decorated or learning Russian or finishing the home study. I was lying in my bed one night staring at the ceiling and thinking, I am going to Khabarovsk in mid-May and start the adoption, for real, finally. I felt a heady mixture of fear and excitement.

I had told some close friends about the adoption, but not everyone in my wide circle of friends and family members. However, I felt more and more strongly with every day that passed, that this was a prayer-driven venture. I was awed by how much had been accomplished against such great odds. Late one night I sent an e-mail to every friend, family member, and acquaintance for which I could find an address, telling them of my adoption and asking them to pray

I received many supportive replies. I was so grateful to everyone. I have always believed prayer can work miracles.

On April 10, I got an e-mail from Kate saying that her aunt had delivered the latest box of gifts to Alesia at the orphanage and that Alesia was very happy. She said the other girls told her Alesia's mother never visits and that she misses her very much. I thought about it all day. This is the text of Kate's message:

My aunt took the package to Alesia yesterday (it was Thursday in Khabarovsk).

Here is what my aunt said:

Yesterday I took the package to the orphan house. They fixed up the orphan house. It is clean. Alesia was very happy. Girls came running and gathered around me. They were all very nice looking and looked mature. I understood that this orphan house was for older children. Alesia lived in Vinogradovka before, she told me. Small children live there.

She told me that her mother doesn't visit her. She misses her a lot and that she doesn't remember her face. I didn't really understand but I think she had lived at home for about 5 or 6 years until her mother was taken her custody rights away. Alesia is 12 now. She is very small and thin. I would think that she looks more like 8 or 9. Other girls are probably 12 too, this is why I thought that they looked

mature. I talked to the girls for a little bit while I was waiting for
Alesia. They went looking for Alesia. She was taking the dogs out.
Girls told me that she likes dogs very much and likes to walk them.
She walks far.

Alesia said that she would write to Dee. She is waiting for her
very much and can't wait till she is taken from there.

Alesia may need some counseling to deal with grief issues,
I thought. I couldn't imagine being six years old and being taken
away from my mother. It would have been devastating. (I later
learned that many older adopted children swallow this grief and
pain, and do not process it for years. A good therapist is essential
to processing the pain and healing from their traumatic pasts.)

I spent Easter weekend at my mother's house in Augusta. I
had spent about twenty-four hours visiting her. She was sad
because she had to have her old dog, Maggie, put to sleep. I had
cried all afternoon on Thursday when she told me about it.
Maggie was a big shaggy mutt dog—a wonderful companion to
my mother after my father died.

I missed Richard so much on Easter Sunday. I hated not
seeing him on a holiday. New Jersey seemed very far away, even
though we spoke on the phone nearly every day. Seeing him one
weekend a month wasn't really enough, but it was all we could
manage.

I spent a lot of time on the Yahoo message boards for parents
adopting from Russia, and a couple of other message boards for
adoptive parents. Some of the advice on there was good, some
was not. I just had a hunger to read everything I could about
adoption and to hear about other folks' experiences.

April 16 was a momentous day for me. I sent off the first

packet of Russian dossier documents, including the notarized home study. I spent my lunch hour running around town, first to get two different copies of my birth certificate—with real signatures, not stamped ones. Then I had to go to the agency and pick up my home studies, including certified copies of the agency's license and a letter verifying they would do my post-adoption placements. Then I had to go to a different office and get everything apostilled [it validates a notary seal for a foreign government], then rush back to the office to get everything in the Fed-Ex package place before 2:00 p.m.

I finally sat down to eat my lunch at 1:30 and I thought, I so want to hug my mother or my boyfriend right now. I want so much to share this moment with somebody who will know why I have these tears in my eyes—because I am a big step closer to my dream of having a family. I sent an e-mail instead. It was the best I could manage.

Masha e-mailed a few days later and said she needed more copies of photos of me with people (I had sent only photos of my home) and a letter about the local agency's license renewal. So I ran around and got all that, got the letter apostilled, and also got the visa application filled out and off to the travel agency. (All foreign travelers to Russia must have a visa.) I hoped that within the next week or so I would know my travel dates in May and have my visa in hand.

My efforts to learn Russian were progressing slowly. I listened to my Russian CD every morning while I exercised, but found it harder and harder to listen to the CD's in the car with the travel vocabulary. I realized that I needed some mental "down" time each day when I didn't think about the adoption.

April 22 was a great day. I got an e-mail from Kate, with two translated letters from Alesia thanking us for her Easter presents. She also included several cute drawings, one of which showed me (Mama Dee), Alesia, and Babushka (grandmother) Elva. Alesia's hair was in pigtails in the drawing and she stood between us. We all had on purple shoes. She also sent a drawing of a table with a samovar and Easter foods on it, and some sketches of Easter eggs. I printed all of them in color and put them up in my cubicle at work.

Here are Alesia's letters:

Dear Grandmother Elva,
I have learned to love you. I am glad that you are Dee's mother. I will be your granddaughter. It is so wonderful. I never have been with a grandmother. I think we will see each other often when I am in America. I can't wait for it too. I always wanted to have a family. I think that I will really like the bedroom that you prepared for me. I don't have a favorite food but I like some things more than others. They are simple, the ones that they give us here at the orphan house. I think I will eat everything with pleasure whatever you cook for me. I wear various clothes but I have very little clothes at this time. I have a dress. Some girls buy their own clothes but I don't have a passport and I cannot work.

Thank you very much for the Easter presents. I shared candies with the girls. I liked toys and clothes for Barbie. I wore a blouse to school once. It is very comfortable. Thank you again.

Dear Dee, I am very glad to get to know your mother. She is as kind as you are. I hope you had a nice Easter. Mine was nice. Thank you very much for the presents and vitamins. Especially that they are so needed now. They are interesting and tasty too. Some kids and I (14 people) went to the All-Russian Competition in skiing, checkers-

chess, volleyball and relay race from the 23rd of March through the
2nd of April. We went from Khabarovsk to Ulan-Ude for 2.5 days by
train. Our team won the 3rd place.
The last semester just started. I am trying hard. I got two A's on
the 10th of April for Life Safety and Biology. I can't wait till the day
that I can see and hug you. I miss you very much.
> *With big love, Your daughter Alesia.*
> *Happy Easter to Dee and Elva.*

In some ways she sounded much younger than 12 years old,
I thought. There was also a card that she made. It said (and it
rhymed in Russian):

Mama Dee,
I wish you to blossom and be healthy
It is very important for the future life
Let every day bring something new to you
Let the heart beat in your chest be the kind one
And there is one more card that she made for Elva:
Grandmother Elva, I wish you joy and happiness. I wish that you
smile a lot. I wish you to always be beautiful.

I immediately called Mom and told her to check her e-mail.
I told her why. She said "OK, 'Bye," and hung up. A record short
conversation for Mom! She was thrilled when she read the letter,
she told me later.

I had a big world map on the wall of my cubicle and I
looked up Ulan Ude, a city west of Khabarovsk. I didn't know
they would let the orphans travel like that. I was pleased to see
that Alesia had gotten out in the outside world a little bit and had
seen other places. I hoped that would make her traveling to

America a little easier.

Mom proudly displayed Alesia's drawing of the three of us on her fridge. After I put it up on the wall of my cubicle at work, I looked at it often. I was so pleased with how carefully Alesia had drawn everything. It was obvious that she was a talented artist.

On April 29, I was finally able to make solid travel plans. Khabarovsk is a two-trip region, and the first trip required a lot of planning, since I wasn't with a big group like the choir where all the arrangements were made for us. I worked with a travel agency on the west coast which had been recommended by the agency.

I wrote in my journal:

So I will see Alesia in about 20 days! I can't wait to see her. I must redouble my energy in learning some Russian. I hope I can take her shopping for some clothes while I am there, or at least perhaps buy her some things and give to her. I also hope I can either arrange for someone to tutor her in English or buy her some tapes or something. She is studying it, but she needs to really try hard, now.

By early May the pace of activities had really quickened. I spent most of the day May 2 getting photos copied and I finished organizing Alesia's photo album.

A few days later, I learned there was an event in Khabarovsk the days I was going to be there and I couldn't get a room at the Hotel Amethyst where I had planned to stay. Everything I tried online showed no availability. I hated the thought of having to change the dates I traveled, but I couldn't really stay at a private home (Kate's aunt, for example), because foreigners who want to stay with Russians have to register their passport and get permission, which the government doesn't want to give—a huge hassle. I prayed about it a lot.

In May, problems with Richard surfaced. I recorded this in my journal:

I haven't heard from my long-distance boyfriend in a few days. I sent him an e-mail the other day asking him to tell me how he feels about me—always a scary thing to guys. He has always acted loving and caring in the months we've seen each other, but lately he cuts off the conversations when I start talking about going to Russia. I don't know why.

I am bad about writing e-mails that I shouldn't write—it's always easier to confront a person in writing rather than face-to-face. I realized after I wrote Richard the e-mail that I shouldn't have sent it, even though I tried to be very careful in choosing my words. I couldn't get him to talk about feelings when we were together, so I hoped that maybe he would write what he felt. In the beginning of our relationship, he had written me great e-mails. They stopped after we started speaking on the phone all the time. He knew he had won me and didn't have to woo me—that was what I figured.

Another part of my mind kept thinking, though, that we could work out whatever problems we had. I just felt so strongly that Richard was meant to be my life partner. But I had a struggle getting him to talk to me about anything meaningful.

In early May, Kate was able to use her connections in Khabarovsk and get a hotel room for me. What a relief!

I got a sweet letter from a friend of Mom's, an older lady named Dot who lived in Augusta. She never married or had children. She was in her late seventies. Her letter was so kind. I had been meaning to write her a thank-you note, but didn't get it done. Mom sent me this e-mail:

Just want to tell you that Miss Dorothy called. She said she had told her pastor about you and Alisha. Last night, he prayed a special prayer, calling y'all by name during the regular service. People stopped after church and asked about you. One man, a lawyer, said he could put you in touch with a lawyer who does lots of foreign adoptions. Her friend's name is Ed. People want to help. Dot never married and she said tonight that if single women could have adopted when she was younger, she'd have been first in line.

I reflected on how sad I would be if I couldn't adopt a child just because I am single. Thirty or more years ago, a single woman was expected to remain childless, and adoption wasn't an option. It just wasn't done. Thank God the world has come such a long way since Miss Dot was young. I wrote Miss Dot a thank-you note, actually a fairly long one, typed. Thank God I type fast. I was up until after 11:00. I felt like it was important, though. I was so touched that her church was praying for me.

By mid May, many people had sent notes and photos to Alesia. My cousin Jan sent her a journal for her to write her feelings, a United States coloring book, and a lovely note welcoming her to the family. Other cousins came through with letters and photos.

Mom came to visit for the weekend. I was proud she had driven herself—interstates make her nervous. She brought skirts and dresses for me to wear to the orphanage. I wanted to look nice, since people in Russia dress much more formally than here—at least outside Moscow. You don't see many people wearing jeans or sweat clothes.

Sunday May 10th was Mother's Day. Mom and I went to Kate's house (about 45 minutes away) in Acworth to pick up a suitcase she was letting me borrow and some gifts she was sending to friends and family in Khabarovsk. Kate and her mother had prepared a wonderful traditional Russian meal. There were about seven vegetable dishes. We brought several things, too. The best and most interesting food was a dish that is sort of like chicken won ton soup, cooked in little pots with dough over the top—pilmeni. It was delicious. Kate had grown tomatoes, as well as many of the vegetables. Then we looked at photos and just chatted. Everything was really nice, even though Kate's mother didn't speak English. Kate's interpreting was as natural as breathing, so that helped. I had also learned to say *It's delicious* in Russian, and I said it a lot.

I missed Richard. I called him on the cell phone. He had sent his mother a dozen roses for Mother's Day. I wished so much that he could be with me. Hearing his voice made me miss him more.

By mid May, I hardly had time to breathe. I was trying to finish up the photo album, put in all the translations of captions, pack, and buy gifts. I fell into bed every night with my mind racing.

Work was going well, I thought. I wasn't busy. I was still having a hard time working with Peter, who only wanted to give me clerical work, however, not actual paralegal work. Madeline never had time to talk to me about it.

In hindsight, I should've been more proactive about trying to resolve the situation at work. At the time, however, I just wanted to coast a bit. I did my assignments and just tried to avoid conflicts.

I couldn't think about anything much except going to Russia and seeing Alesia. She had become the primary focus of my life.

Chapter Eleven

THE FIRST ADOPTION TRIP

By Saturday, May 15, the frenzy was over. All the lists, the planning, and the packing were all done and I was on my way. Sitting in the airport, I kept thinking of things I had forgotten to do. I had set the security alarm, but forgot to hide my jewelry and credit cards, forgot to close the blinds and unplug the curling iron as a precaution, etc. I kept reviewing in my mind how the stove looked when I wiped it off at 9:25—no lights on, right?

My friend Ricky took me to the airport. On the way, Ricky had to stop at the Quik Trip and get gas. I looked around thinking, Goodbye USA and all you people who are so lucky to live here. I'm off to the land of squatty potties and cigarette-smelly air.

My first stop was Moscow to spend the night and break up the trip. I had no problems in customs or getting my baggage. The hotel was lovely, very American, a Holiday Inn. It was not right in town but had a shuttle to town. I slept a lot the first night and spent the next day, a Monday, shopping in town. I had time to kill since my plane for Khabarovsk didn't leave until that night.

My shopping trip into Moscow wasn't too successful, but it was quite an adventure. I only found a few gifts, and never found the "Gum" department store. I kept wandering the streets and found a lot of bookstores and department stores, but no place selling souvenirs.

I walked around for nearly four hours. I wore a horrible blister on the back of my left heel. When I got back, took off my shoes and saw the sock had a huge bloodstain on it, I had a moment of panic. How do I get antibiotic ointment in Russia, I wondered.

After eating dinner, getting to the airport, and a very long nine-hour flight, finally I got to Khabarovsk. I was met by an agency representative, Zina.

Like the hotel shuttle driver, Zina drove like a New York cabbie—this must be how all Russians drive, I thought. She could qualify for the *Indy 500*, but she was not as bad as the Moscow shuttle driver. He was charged by testosterone, I suppose. Zina had a car seat in her car for her four year old daughter—I guess that's why she drove a bit slower.

Khabarovsk in the spring was lovely and awful, just like Moscow. Beautiful trees, including the tall birches, lined the road. A lot of open ground was covered in trash, though. The buildings ranged from shabby and scary tenement to beautiful, old, historic, and gorgeous. There were some flowers out. The sun made it hot, but not Atlanta hot.

The hotel was nice by Khabarovsk standards, bizarre by American standards. It was situated between two ramshackle tenement-looking apartment buildings. The lobby was tiny. There were gambling machines to one side and a small front desk to the other side. The clerk didn't appear to speak English, but then again Zina took charge of the check-in. I got coupons to pay for my breakfast, since the price was included in the room.

I hardly had time to get in and throw down my bags when the phone rang. It was Larissa, Kate's friend. She said she and Toma (Kate's aunt) would be there in thirty minutes! Yikes. No time to shower, though I desperately wanted to do so. I ran and put their presents on the sofa. I had a small sitting room and a bedroom.

Kate had sent them a lot of things. I had brought each of them things, too, to thank them for all their kindness.

I put in my contacts and slapped on some makeup, trying

not to sweat. It was hot—probably eighty degrees, with sun heating up the room. No air conditioner. I opened the window. No screens.

Ten minutes later, a knock. I opened the door and was immediately hugged and hugged some more by both Larissa, a petite blonde and Toma, an older, attractive motherly-looking lady. Larissa spoke some English, pretty well in fact, but Toma did not. Both exclaimed and chattered in Russian. Larissa had brought some antibiotic cream for my blistered foot, thank God, and some bandaids. Kate had emailed her. The foot looked like it might gangrene at any moment.

We were driven to the restaurant by Larissa's daughter's boyfriend, Aloysha. Larissa said he spoke English, but his English was hesitant. The car was tiny, the steering wheel again on the British side. He didn't drive quite as wildly as most Russians. We got to the restaurant, which was in the Sapporo Hotel. We had to hike up three steep flights of steps. No elevator. I sweated some more. We were shown into a small private dining room with a fairly large table and a good sized window, which was open. There were chopsticks on the table, but also forks.

Larissa's friend Irina met us there. She was a translator, and translated all evening—a very nice lady. Irina lived in Komsomolsk, about a five hour drive north. She had been to Khabarovsk to visit her daughter, who was expecting a baby. She said she was only forty-five and ready to become a grandmother —just a few years older than I.

Dinner was a mixture of cold vegetable dishes and hot dishes. There were petite bowls of rice. The portions were tiny, by American standards. After we had eaten about everything on the table, Toma said, "They didn't bring us enough food. Hardly any meat!" She ordered another meat dish—beef in a hibachi, which was very good. It was put in the middle of the table. They also brought ice cream at the same time.

A funny misinterpretation occurred. When the waitress brought the beef dish, she placed a small dish of what looked like lemon sauce between Toma and me and indicated that we should dip the beef in it. I tried it and it was good. Of course, I was talking a mile a minute. At about the third bite, I realized that the bland yellow sauce was raw egg! Yikes! A salmonella panic. No more of that for me. Irina noticed my horrified face and I explained that in America we don't eat raw eggs.

The meal was comical, for a couple of reasons. All three of these women were professional women and each had a cell phone. About every five minutes, one of the cell phones would ring. This reminded me of home. Another funny thing was that they all fussed over me like mother hens, telling me to try this, drink that, etc. You would have thought I was pregnant.

When the evening was winding down, I told Irina (the interpreter) that I wanted to tell them the story of Alesia. Irina did a great job interpreting. I told them about the dream, about meeting Alesia, about crying when I had to leave her behind. By the time I finished they all looked like THEY were going to cry. It was really a nice and funny moment. They were all mothers and could relate.

During dinner, Toma said something so sad. She said Alesia came from a small settlement, Pobeda, that was not far away from the orphanage, maybe an hour. The other girls had told her, however, that it was a long way away, too far for her mom to come for a visit, to lessen the pain caused by Alesia's family never coming to see her. Poor baby.

The next morning, after a night of being bitten by insects, since there were no window screens, I was exhausted and ready for breakfast. I had also been kept awake by the sound of snoring next door.

I went downstairs to the hotel restaurant. There were many choices for breakfast. Among them were pancakes stuffed with meat and rice. Another breakfast choice was fried eggs. I tried to get them, but with tea instead of coffee. "Nyet," I was told sternly. I sat down to wait and was given a glass of warm bubbly mineral water.

My breakfast was variant number nine, two small cheese muffin-like pancakes with sour cream, two pieces of bread, two small squares of cheese, and a cup of tea. While I ate, I looked around. There were about six Russian men at the other little ice-cream parlor tables. They were all dressed in suits and ties. I wondered which one had been the obnoxious snorer I heard all night.

I had time to kill before I could go to the orphanage to see Alesia. She was in school until 1:00, then back at the orphanage for lunch.

The rest of the morning was spent visiting with some missionaries I had met in 2003. I also had lunch with Olga Volnycheva, an English teacher I had met when the choir was there.

Olga agreed to walk down to the nearby City Market with me, though it made her uncomfortable—she said there were many pickpockets there. There were many booths, like a flea market, but the range of goods was more like a mall. There was a lot of cheap stuff—cosmetics, plastic stuff, cheap clothes and shoes. There were also fresh fruits and vegetables, like a farmers market. Oddest of all, to me, was the amazing variety of shiny chrome plumbing fixtures—a lot of faucets, etc.—all piled on a table. I did find a couple of pretty nesting dolls which were hand-painted, and bought them for friends.

Olga asked around and found out the name of a nearby café and we walked there, to the café Samovar. It was really not a café, but a small cafeteria. There was very little choice in foods—I picked a dish of chicken and rice and a Sprite. Olga and I had a good chat, and I told her my plan to ask about Alesia having private English lessons. I wanted Olga to teach her some English before she came to America but I had to get agency approval.

I got back to the hotel and just had time to change into a dress and makeup. Anya (the main coordinator for the agency's program in Khabarovsk) and her two assistants (including Zina) took me out to the orphanage.

I was rather taken aback by the dress of the assistants. The tall assistant, Marina, had on silvery colored hip-huggers and a silver shirt that showed her midriff. She also had on a lot of makeup. Zina was also colorfully dressed. They had really different standards of business attire in Russia, at least for women. Zina, whose hair was dyed red, had on black pointy-toed laceup boots, and a red leather jacket, which she kept on all the time. They would look odd in America but they looked right at home there.

On the other hand, Anya, who was their boss, looked normal and dressed a lot more conservatively. She had on slacks and a shirt. Except for her oddly dyed red hair, she would have looked right at home in an American supermarket.

We got to the orphanage at about 2:00. It was a really ugly, depressing looking place on the outside. I had not seen it in daylight when the choir was there. The yard was bare dirt with sketchy patches of grass. There was a nice swing set but no other play equipment. Danny Griffin's church group had built the swing set the previous summer.

The moment the car stopped in the little side parking area,

I saw Alesia walking, about ten feet away. She looked at the cars, but turned and walked away, disinterested. She doesn't know it's me, I thought, heart pounding.

I got out of the car, trying to remain calm, and walked behind her. I called her name. She turned and stared at me for a moment, blankly. I said her name again and smiled. Recognition, then, finally. She shouted "Dee!" and ran, throwing herself into my arms. Her oversized, raggedy clothes and gaunt body made me want to weep.

I hugged her and spoke softly in Russian, "Hello. How are you? Are you well?" I was trying to keep it low key. I didn't cry. It was a happy moment.

Alesia finally pulled away and looked into my face with a big grin. She looked like she had grown since I last saw her, but that had been almost a year and a half before. She was dressed in an old skirt and shirt, an oversized boy's coat, and blue bedroom slippers. She looked like a ragamuffin, but her beaming face told me she was happy to see me. That's all I really noticed.

We first went into the orphanage and Anya asked to be shown to the social worker on site. Her tiny office was crammed with Anya, Alesia, Marina, Zina, and me. Anya and the social worker had a heated exchange in Russian and finally went outside.

I talked to Alesia a little, with Marina and Zina translating. Alesia was shy and didn't want to look at me. I think she just felt strange and "on stage," which was not typical for her.

It startled me when Zina said to her in Russian that she could call me "Mama"—I caught that word because it's the same in both languages and immediately asked her what she had said. She repeated it in English. I was horrified. I said, "Please tell Alesia that she can call me whatever she likes, and if she wants to call me Dee, that's fine." I could tell the whole exchange made Alesia uncomfortable. (I later thought about it, and realized that her "Mama" never visited her and that she might have only negative associations with that word.)

Alesia was sent off while we had several meetings with folks in the orphanage. The orphanage director wasn't there, but I left the gift I had bought him with his assistant. I thought it was strange that he wasn't there. Anya had told him I would be coming.

We first spoke to a female medical doctor who worked in the orphanage. Her office looked like it had been frozen in time in the 1950's—glass cases, stainless steel containers, and wooden furniture. It was so tiny that Anya, Zina, and I sat on the examining table. My feet didn't touch the floor. The doctor basically said that Alesia had no major medical problems and was not positive for TB. She said Alesia had some gallbladder problems and couldn't eat foods that were spicy or fatty, but that she had no need for medication. I decided to make sure that her pediatrician at home checked out all that.

I asked what I thought was a perfectly reasonable question about FAS (Fetal Alcohol Syndrome). I figured the odds were that Alesia might have it, since she came from a family of alcoholics. "Anya, ask the doctor if she sees any signs of Fetal Alcohol exposure in Alesia," I said evenly. Instead of translating my question, Anya immediately yelled, "Why would you say that! Does she LOOK like an imbecile?!"

I was shocked by Anya's outburst. I said something to the effect that no, she certainly doesn't look like that, but she said her mother was an alcoholic, and that I thought it was a legitimate question. Glaring at me, Anya finally asked the doctor. "No, I have not seen signs of that," the doctor said.

I sighed. "Look, even if Alesia does have FAS, I will still

adopt her." I could feel Anya's eyes boring into me from the right side. I couldn't look at her. I was so irritated. It was an awkward moment, to say the least.

We next spoke to the social worker. She had not wanted to talk to us and Anya argued a lot with her, finally showing her a paper signed by some official saying we were allowed to be there. She gave me very little information, which was frustrating. I had thought I would get a copy of the file, but I was told I would only get that after the adoption was final—I could ask her questions, though. Haltingly, shuffling repeatedly through papers, the woman threw out tidbits of information.

"Alesia has been at Topolevo since 1998. Her father was alive in 1998, but his parental rights were terminated because of abandonment. Her mother simply neglected Alesia." I nodded. None of that surprised me. I asked if the grandparents were alive. The woman looked through papers some more and read. Finally, she said, "The grandparents were old (in Russia, that could mean anything over 40) and didn't have the money to be able to take in Alesia."

I asked specifically if it said there that Alesia's mother or grandmother was alcoholic, but there was no mention of it. However, I tend to believe Alesia had told me the truth on that, since she lived there until she was almost seven years old.

"Alesia's mother lived only off the money the government gave her to care for Alesia. She didn't work...The mother did, at least, attend the hearing to terminate her parental rights. She admitted she had no job..."

Obviously the mother didn't care enough about Alesia to get a job and try to get her back.

I asked if there was evidence of child abuse and was told no. I asked if the mother or grandmother could step in and interfere with the adoption and was told no. That was a relief.

The file included a small photo of Alesia at age seven, which was very cute. It looked like a school picture. She had short, curly blonde hair. I asked if I could have a copy of that. "Nyet," I was informed. (No.)

Finally, the woman looked up from her file, rubbed her eyes, and put down her glasses. She spoke in Russian, slowly, looking at me intently. After a moment, Anya translated.

"She said that Alesia, unlike all the other kids in the orphanage, has never had a letter from her mother or father or grandparents. They have never called. They have never visited. This is unusual, with older kids. It's like her family forgot about her." I just nodded, trying not to cry. My poor girl. There was an awkward pause.

I finally thought to ask the social worker if I could bring in a teacher to tutor Alesia in English, and she said she would ask, but that it should be fine.

After the formal interviews, Anya and Marina left and went back to town. Zina stayed with me to translate while I visited with Alesia.

Alesia showed me her room. It was a large room with beautiful lace curtains across the large windows. There were ten very small beds, cots really, covered with old, faded brown flowered spreads. Against a wall, there were ten tiny cabinets where the kids put their possessions, not much bigger than a typical school locker.

The beds had pillows mounded up into triangular shapes, which looked very odd to me. I asked Zina about it and she obviously didn't understand my question, because she just said, "They want the beds to look neat."

Off the bedroom there was a small study room with desks,

and some shelving that held games and a few toys. The toys looked dirty and worn out.

After seeing the room and passing out some candy to the kids, I thought that we should go outside. I felt bad that I didn't have gifts for all ten little girls in Alesia's group. I gave her some small bottles of moisturizer and told her to share them with the others.

We went back down the ramshackle staircase and ascended two flights to the heavy door that looked like it belonged on a barn.

Zina and I walked outside with Alesia. The other kids were not out there. I talked to her, Zina translating. It was kind of awkward. Alesia was a bit shy, still, so I didn't want to have any heavy conversations with her.

I wasn't sure if Alesia really understood about the adoption. I explained, "You will leave Russia and take a long flight across the ocean. You will live with me and be my daughter. You will have your own room. You will go to school."

Alesia sat down on what looked like an old wooden cross-beam, laying in the yard. She grabbed a stick and drew in the dirt.

I told her "I want you to learn English, and I will try to arrange for a tutor for you. The more you know, the easier it will be to adjust to America."

Alesia looked up at Zina and said something, softly. Zina explained, "She said she is made to learn German in school." Well, that sure doesn't help, I thought.

"Sweetie, will you try to learn English, try your best?"

Alesia nodded.

"Alesia, I cannot take you with me on this trip, but I will come back this summer and get you, OK?"

Alesia nodded again. "And then we will go on the airplane?"

"Da," I answered. (Yes.)

We left around 5:00 and Zina drove me back to the hotel.

That night, I actually got more than eight hours sleep. I felt lucky that I didn't get any mosquito bites. I couldn't shower because there was no hot water at 9:00 A.M.—there was not even any tepid water, which I could stand. I had to just squat in the tub and wash my hair and a few other vital areas, and I nearly froze.

Then, while dressing, I had wet hair because there was no hair dryer in the room. The window was open because there is no air conditioner. People in America have no idea how lucky they are.

While dressing, I thought about the girls I had seen in the orphanage. Several had been lying on their beds with their heads under their pillows. Not even my presence roused them. I just wanted to hug each of them and tell them it will be all right—but it knew it wouldn't. When they leave the orphanage they have very little chance of a decent future. They may become criminals or prostitutes, like many orphans. Many also commit suicide— one statistic I read was that ten percent kill themselves in the first year after they leave the orphanage. I pondered that as I fell asleep, again hot and miserable.

The next morning I had the exact same breakfast as the day before. Then I fled back to the room. I had to cry for a while. The events of the past few days had suddenly overwhelmed me. I missed my family, my friends, Richard, my mother. As I sat in the chair sobbing, I kept thinking, how can those poor children bear not having parents to love them? I could not imagine growing up that way.

My afternoon at the orphanage was totally different.

It began with my showing Alesia the scrapbook of notes from other kids and the photo album. We were sitting in a little schoolroom off the bedroom. She was clearly fascinated, and looked sometimes awed when she read the captions in Russian. I doubt she had ever been connected to America in quite that way. She only knew America from movies!

After a few minutes, Anya brought in a middle-aged lady and introduced her as an education ministry official who wanted to observe me with Alesia and ask me some questions. She was a drab, slightly overweight woman. She looked at the photo album very carefully. She only asked me a few questions—where would Alesia's school be, would they teach her English, why did I want to adopt Alesia particularly, etc. She spoke to Alesia very kindly, and I think asked her if she wanted to go to America and be adopted. "Da!" was the answer. (Yes)

At one point, the official and all the agency women—Marina, Anya, and Zina—were all sitting around the small table. All had seen the photo album. All were talking in rapid Russian to Alesia. I had no idea what was being said. I finally asked Zina what was going on. She explained that they were talking about Alesia's future. Alesia said she wanted to be either a model or a veterinarian.

I said, "Tell her that in America models have to be very tall."

Zina said yes, but she could grow, and she is very thin and pretty. I said, "Yes, she is thin now, but when her grandmother starts feeding her she won't be very thin any more!" Zina translated it and all the women laughed.

I spent some time talking to one of Alesia's caretakers, who seemed to be a caring person, my age or younger. She was a shy, plain young woman wearing jeans and a fuzzy brown turtleneck. She had short brown hair and no makeup, unlike most young

Russian women. She said mostly what I already knew—that Alesia liked being outdoors, liked animals, tried hard, was obedient, etc. Then silence.

Hesitantly, she said, "Alesia gets very emotional sometimes."

I nodded. I said, "That's okay, I do too," and smiled. "I will get her any counseling she needs to adjust to America."

I was amazed to learn how sheltered Alesia had been. The caretaker said Alesia had been once to a movie theatre, but had never eaten in a restaurant. I knew I would ponder that later.

I got to know some of the other girls in Alesia's group. They were cute and funny. I spent the rest of the afternoon playing games and talking to the girls (through Zina, who translated).

We played Simon Says, which they all thought was very funny. I did a lot of funny moves, like the twist, the swim, etc. There was a lot of giggling. Snezhana and a little girl named Oxana were the best players. A little later they said, "Do something funny, Dee!"

The only negative moment came at about 5:30 when we were leaving. We were standing in the little study room, and a big bald man barged in. The girls were immediately cowed.

He spoke harshly to Zina. She immediately got upset. They spoke Russian for a minute. Then Zina said to me, "We have to go."

After he left, I asked her who the man was, though I already knew. He was the orphanage director, she said, and he had just hit her car in the parking area. We walked outside and looked at her car, which indeed had a dent in it, though not too big. It was driveable.

Zina and the director talked a while. She called her husband on the cell phone. The director never once said anything to me. When we drove out onto the highway from the road in front of the orphanage, he was sitting in his car, his head down on the steering wheel, looking sleepy. It was very strange.

Back at the hotel, I went downstairs to the restaurant and ate a bowl of soup, called something like "Salonka." It was okay, not great. I wasn't hungry. All I could think about were the girls at the orphanage.

The next morning, Svitlana (the missionary) showed up at the hotel and we spent some time talking. Her English had improved a lot. I tried to keep my words as simple as possible, however. I gave her a monetary donation for her ministry.

We talked about her ministry and looked at her photos. She ministered to more than seven hundred children in ten different orphanages. I told her how much I admired her dedication.

As soon as she left, Anya picked me up. We went to the office of a notary and I signed an official paper. The notary was an older woman whose office was very nice, by Russian standards. There were beautiful white lace curtains and a lot of plants. She also had a very modern looking computer. Anya explained that now Alesia could not be adopted by anyone else. I looked out at the drab, rainy weather, and it didn't matter at all. I was a step closer to getting Alesia home. Hallelujah!

On the way back, Anya and I had to stop by a bank and get rubles in exchange for one of the $100 bills I had given her. It had a few tiny pinholes in it and Anya couldn't get it cashed. The bank was a small drab room, and had no tellers like an American bank, just a window in a wall. It reminded me of a convenience store in a bad neighborhood. Anya spoke in rapid-fire Russian to a woman on the other side. I gave the $100 bill to the bank teller with my passport and got back the rubles.

Anya also explained to me that on Monday she had gone to the orphanage and spoken to the director and everyone about my visit. However, they were so unused to anyone adopting the children that they didn't know what to do and she had to explain it all. She told them we were coming on Wednesday, but they all acted surprised when we got there. That's why she argued so much with everyone—the doctor, social worker, assistant director.

Anya also said that the inexperience of the Topolevo folks means that I would not be able to get Alesia in July or August as I had hoped. Many court employees took vacations in August. I was upset to hear that. I had to not think about it or I would cry.

When I got back to the hotel I spent some time packing carefully. I had gifts that were fragile, so I tried to wrap everything carefully in dirty clothes. The duffel bag of Kate's was much lighter than when I arrived. I prayed that nothing would get broken.

As I packed, I grieved over the thought that I wouldn't have Alesia home in the summer. I had so wanted to celebrate her July birthday with her. I had wanted her to get extra help with English before starting school. Anya's cavalier attitude about the summer slowdown and the adoption being delayed until fall was unreal to me. She acted like it was no big deal my child would have to stay in an orphanage for several extra months, just because some bureaucrat took the whole month of August off for vacation!

The next day, Friday, Olga came to the hotel at noon and we had lunch. We each had soup. I also had French fries.   I gave Olga the money for teaching Alesia—fourteen lessons at $20 each, in rubles. She talked about getting books and tapes to help Alesia.

She asked about Alesia's background, and I told her what the social worker had told me. She looked aghast and quickly said, "I will ask to bring her to my home!" (for the weekend). This was very nice of her. I said I wasn't sure if it would be allowed, but she could try.

Olga promised to explain to Alesia how different American and Russian schools are—her grandson lived in America and she had visited his school.

While we were chatting, a hotel clerk handed me a cordless phone, and it was Anya. She said they had called and learned my flight to Moscow had been postponed until the next day, Saturday morning at 9:00! So that meant an extra night in Khabarovsk. Anya had already arranged with the hotel to let me have an extra night there.

Zina picked me up at 1:30 and we went out to the orphanage. Alesia ran up and gave me a hug as soon as we stepped out of the car. She was wearing (for the third day) the same pink shirt I had given her on the first day. Her hair was pulled back in an untidy ponytail. I explained that I needed to go back to the hotel—I had completely forgotten the gifts.

Alesia looked sad that I had to turn around and leave. I reassured her I would be right back.

I insisted Zina take me back to the hotel to get the gifts, because I wanted to give them to Alesia personally. I wanted to explain to Alesia about some special gifts from my cousins, and see how she did with the little basic English words and pictures books I brought. I explained to Alesia several times that I would return soon—it was only a fifteen minute drive back to the hotel.

We drove back to the hotel and I got the books and put them in Zina's car. We decided to buy some cakes at the grocery store next door to the hotel and take them to the girls for a party.

Traditional Russian grocery stores are just large rooms with glass cases all around the perimeter. There is little to buy. There are stern-looking ladies behind the counters. You have to ask for everything, even the few fruits and vegetables.

The cakes were in one case that looked like a typical bakery case, but there were only a few of them. They were all round—no square cakes there. We bought two little cakes, juice, and spoons and plates. The spoons and plates were sold individually. The cakes had somewhat bizarre decorations and fruit fillings.

The girls were glad to see us return with the food. They got glasses from the kitchen for the juice and a knife for the cakes. They pushed the desks together in the little study room to form a sort of table.

As soon as we got there I realized I had to use the bathroom. I zipped in the doorway to the bathroom the girls used and stopped, horrified. It was a dank, dirty, dingy room with cement floors. There were two small white porcelain sinks. There were two toilets, but not in booths—they were separated from the sinks by only a flimsy curtain. There was no toilet paper. They were using cheap paperback book pages and throwing the used wads into a wastebasket. (I pitied the poor person who had to empty that.) I saw no tub or shower. Each girl had a small towel on a hook. I used my liquid hand sanitizer.

When I got back to the schoolroom, the girls were sitting politely, waiting for us to eat first. I told Zina I wanted her to translate and I would say a blessing—I don't usually say a blessing for a snack but I wanted the girls to know we bless our food. Zina was very startled that I asked, but reluctantly translated. She kept looking at me like I was crazy. I later found out that most Russians think people who believe in God are crazy—a holdover from communist times.

Zina's behavior didn't bother the kids. They all ate politely. They offered some cake to the other girls from a different group who lived next door.

The girls told Zina that, while we were gone, Alesia had

stood in the rain outside waiting and watching the whole time, saying, "I miss my Dee!" Bless her heart. Hearing that made me want to cry. The caretaker had said that the first day I showed up at the orphanage, Alesia was sad when I left and very quiet the rest of the day.

After eating cake, I measured Alesia, and traced the outline of her foot. That involved her peeling off two very dirty white socks, and putting her fuzzy bedroom slippers, also dirty, under the nearest bed. Tracing her foot was ticklish. It was obvious she found the process amusing. She giggled a lot. I wanted to be able to fit her properly in clothes and get her some decent tennis shoes.

I showed her the stickers and postcards from my cousin Robin, and the nice diary and coloring book from my cousin Jan. Alesia was pleased with everything.

We also looked at the book from Kate with the nouns (dog, cat, girl, etc.) and the words in English. Alesia was able to read the words very well. I was stunned and thrilled. She was obviously trying her best to learn English. I knew the books would help.

We next played games. I had brought some "prizes"—candy and gum. We played Simon Says. Again, we had great fun with that. I know lots of funny gestures.

Next, I asked if they knew musical chairs, and they knew that game—just not the American name for it. There was a small boombox in the outer living room area, and we used that for musical chairs. The girls loved that game.

I took a lot of photos. I suggested that we go outside, and I got some good shots. The girls wanted Zina in all the photos. They really liked her. She was not that much older than they, and could communicate with them easily.

After a while of taking photos I wanted to go ahead and leave. I dreaded it and wanted to get it over with. We walked over to Zina's car, and the tire was flat! She was not happy, and I don't blame her. I don't know if the kids did it, or if it was an effect from the fender bender the previous day. The car was parked right in front of the orphanage. Fortunately, she had a good spare. Some of the older boys changed the tire for her.

While the tire was being changed, the orphanage director came out and spoke to Zina. He didn't apologize. Once again, he never spoke to me, though he looked at me. I should've introduced myself, but I didn't. He scared me. It was really awkward.

While the tire was being changed, I was surprised to see some of the kids riding bicycles around the yard. I asked Alesia if she knew how to ride a bicycle and she said yes. I told Zina to tell her I would get her a bicycle.

When it finally came time to go, I hugged each of the girls still out there—Sasha, Oxana, Olya, and Snezhana.

Finally, I told Alesia (through Zina) that I would return in August or September, and then we would go to Moscow, then America. She accepted the revised timetable stoically and didn't protest or argue.

I finally pulled her aside and spoke to her alone. I said, in Russian, "My dear daughter, I love you." Then I hugged her. I looked at Zina over Alesia's shoulder and said quietly, "Get me out of here before I cry." We left.

I waved to Alesia from the car and said "Dos Vedanya!" and then thought no, that sounds too final, and I shouted "Pak-ha!" which means "See you later!" I wanted her to be sure and know that I would come back.

As I looked at the muddy orphanage yard and the ragamuffin children, I silently said a prayer for God to take care of them all, especially Alesia. I was proud I didn't cry. I was too overwhelmed, really. Also, I had to admit that the sadness of leaving

Alesia was mixed with relief. I wanted to go home.

That night I had an unexpected visitor to my hotel room—Pasha. He was a young college student who had befriended the choir members on my earlier trip. He speaks fluent English, and is very intelligent and sweet. We had a wonderful time talking that night. I promised to get him some books in English and stay in touch. It made the extra night in Khabarovsk bearable.

The flights the next day were an ordeal. I couldn't spend the night in Moscow as I had planned. Instead, an agency representative met me at the domestic airport and drove me to the international one—a harrowing drive that ignored all traffic rules. I didn't care. I just didn't want to miss my international flight.

The flight from Moscow to Washington was full of adopted babies. I tried not to cry, though seeing them tore at my heart. I so wished Alesia was with me. I chatted with a man in the seat next to me. He was a Russian emigrant, returning to the USA after a visit. He was very sweet. Our conversation was a good distraction. I couldn't sleep.

When I finally got back after being wide awake for over twenty-four hours, I was so thrilled just to be HOME in my little condo. I slept and slept, and dreamed of Alesia being home with me.

Chapter Twelve

HOME TO CHAOS

The end of May 2004 was a stressful time. I was tired from the trip. I hated the thought that Alesia was still in the orphanage. I was impatient to get her home.

I was still not completely over the jet lag. I kept doing absent-minded things all the time, like leaving the kitchen light on all night. I tried not to think too much about leaving Alesia, or I would cry. I kept busy by mailing off little souvenirs to people who had helped me, and sent things for Alesia.

I heard from Masha, and she was very gloomy. She gave me the impression that she and Anya just resented being asked to complete the adoption. Since they were being paid thousands of dollars to help me, I found the attitude very irritating. I needed emotional reassurance. I never got it from anyone connected with the agency. They were barely polite.

Shortly after that, Masha said she was going on vacation. So for three weeks, I heard nothing about the adoption while Masha vacationed. That was irritating. She had no assistant to keep me informed or answer questions. She wouldn't let me e-mail Anya in Khabarovsk. I was beginning to feel she was doing only the minimum to help me. My adoption was completely in her hands and I had no control over the process. I hated that feeling.

I dreamed all the time, vivid and terrible dreams. I started calling them the "school dreams." They had happened after my father died, too. I would be on a campus, one that looked vaguely familiar, but not completely. I would rush off to a class, and get there and have to take a test. I wouldn't remember any of the material. Sometimes I would sit there and realize I had been registered for class but never attended, for some unknown reason. Sometimes I would be looking for my classroom and unable to find it. I think these were just generalized anxiety dreams, but they were really disturbing.

On June 2, there was more bad news. It was several days before I could even write about it. Finally, on June 6, I turned back to my journal:

The last week has been difficult. I spent last weekend in New Jersey with Richard, and I thought things went pretty well. Then he called me a few days ago and said he wanted to change our relationship to "just friends" and not see each other any more. It was a shock. We had a long phone conversation, and I remained calm, which was good. I knew I had erred when I told him I loved him a few weeks ago—he wasn't ready to hear it, and it made him self-conscious and scared him. He pretty much admitted that. I kept my dignity and didn't cry until later, after we had hung up.

I think if this relationship is meant to work out it will, and if not perhaps God has something else in mind for me. I am sort of amazed at how calm I have been, but then again I have Alesia to think about.

The truth, which I couldn't admit to myself until many weeks later, was that I thought it was a temporary breakup. I thought he would miss me after a few weeks, calm down, and we'd get back together. I figured if I just stayed busy and stayed positive and prayed about it, everything would work out. I was sure Richard loved me. I asked a male friend of mine about it, and he said maybe Richard just couldn't handle the long distance relationship, and we'd get back together after he got out of the military in a year and moved back south. I hung onto that hope for a long time.

Rather than focus on missing Richard, I decided to be proactive about trying to find homes for the little girls in Alesia's group. I saw their faces in my mind all the time. I grieved over the fact that I could only adopt one of the group.

I scanned in a photo of all the girls in Alesia's group and sent it out to just about everyone in my address book, with an e-mail urging them to consider adopting one of the girls. I included this:

They do know American culture, a bit. Alesia showed me a photo of Beyonce Knowles and asked me to pronounce her name, and was amazed it was pronounced "bee-ONTS-ay." The interpreter wasn't around, or I would've explained that it's a pretty unusual name in America, too! Alesia also showed me a little photo of the cast of "Charmed" a show they get to see. I asked her if she liked American movies, and she said oh yes, Julia Roberts movies! [Boy is she in for a culture shock...]

I found some puzzles and hair accessories at Target for the girls in Alesia's group. I had also bought games when I was visiting Richard, too—I got Othello (one of my favorites), as well as chess and checkers. At Target, I found Twister. That was one of my favorite games at Alesia's age. I had Kate translate the instructions into Russian.

One thing I knew for sure was that I didn't want to go to Russia alone again for the actual adoption hearing trip. I didn't really feel safe alone in Russia, and when I went back to get Alesia I knew it would be easier with a guy along to help.

I went to see my friend Ricky and his family. Ricky is self-employed as a camera operator—all my other friends worked full-time or were stay-at-home parents. I asked him if he would consider going with me to get Alesia. Ricky and his wife had been very supportive throughout the adoption process and I knew he could make terrific video movies.

I drove out to see Ricky and his wife Hannah one Sunday afternoon and shared the photos from my trip. Ricky and Hannah and their daughter April looked at all my photos carefully, and I think they were then able to understand better how different Alesia's life was in the dismal orphanage. Ricky was enthusiastic about the idea of traveling to Russia. His wife also was supportive and said she could manage without him. I was very relieved to not have to go back alone.

A few days later, I got another really discouraging e-mail from Masha—the worst so far:

Maybe you already had heard that Russian Ministry of Education (among the rest of the Russian government) is undergoing some reorganizing, Federal Data Bank was closed and head of the Bank was fired, so if the inquire for release letter for Olesya which Khabarovsk Regional Department of Education sent to the Federal data Bank wasn't processed before its closing, which we don't know yet, certainly it will be delayed till the Government won't come with new form of organization taking functions of the Federal Data Bank.

Anya discovered in documents she is now working with that Olesya's mother has 2 different names. In birth certificate her last name is Krul, in court decree which terminated her parental rights her name listed as Pavlova. So, right now we have to establish a legal fact through the court that Mrs. Krul and Pavlova are the same person and she is the mother of Olesya. Olesya was born in little village in Khabarovsk region, I guess where we should look for her mother now to work with this new issue. Certainly new legal procedure will delay the process.

I read the e-mail and just cried and cried. I was so fearful. I hated that all this was out of my hands. It was also clear that Masha had a very uncaring attitude.

When I went in to work the next day, I told Peter and Madeline about the delay. I figured they might be glad that I'd go to Russia later in the fall, maybe as late as November.

I was feeling rather "down" the next day about Alesia, about her not coming home until the fall, but I got some comfort from an odd source. I think God sends us messages in interesting ways. There's a Christian song called *I Can Only Imagine* that was occasionally played on the adult contemporary station I listened to. It was just a beautiful song that would make me tear up every time because, although it was about meeting Jesus, it also made me think of bringing Alesia home. It comforted me to hear it.

Often, when I went out at lunch to run errands, it would come on the car radio. In the morning when my alarm went off it was sometimes on the radio. Even though it made me cry, the tears were usually happy ones—I daydreamed of how joyful I would be when I got off the plane and saw my mother and brother at the airport, and how joyous it would be for us to all be together.

To combat the blahs, somewhat at least, I decided to go ahead and write to Alesia and get Kate to translate it. Here is what I wrote:

Dearest Daughter Alesia,

I enjoyed seeing you and talking to you when I was in Khabarovsk. I have gotten my photos developed and will send you copies. Most of the ones I took at the orphanage came out well. Everyone who sees your photo says what a pretty girl you are, and what a great smile you have. (I had gotten a 5x7 made of the best shot of her.)

I tell them I am so lucky and blessed that you will be my daughter.

I loved meeting all the girls who share your room. Each one of them is special and lovely. I look at their photos often. Please give each of them my love and a hug from me. I am telling everyone I know how wonderful the children are at Topolevo, and hoping that adoptive homes can be found. If I could afford it I would adopt more children.

It is getting hot here during the days now, but it's also raining frequently. I have not had a chance to go swimming yet, but I want to. I have a swimming pool here, and my mother has a nice pool. It's usually nice enough weather to swim from April or May until September.

I wish I could tell you exactly when I am returning to Khabarovsk to complete the adoption, but I just don't know. There are several problems that are delaying the adoption, but I can't do anything about them. I trust that God will smooth the way, however, and I will be able to get you in the autumn, if not before. As soon as I know the date when I will return, I will let you know. I am praying for every challenge to be overcome by Anya and the folks at Topolevo working on your adoption. I know they are working hard on our behalf.

I have heard from your English teacher Olga that you are a smart girl—but I knew that already. Please try hard to learn English, and do what Olga asks. She is sending me reports.

There are lots of English words that sound very similar to the Russian words—[Kate insert some words here, maybe 20 common everyday words, OK?].

I am going to send you a Leap Frog and some programs for

your birthday, plus some other things, including things for all the girls in your room. Grandmother Elva will send you something, too.

Do you like the Harry Potter books? Have you read any in Russian?

My birthday is July 4, only a few days before yours. Maybe next year we can celebrate with one big party.

Be good, do what Olga asks. Take your vitamins. Pray every day.

Much Love,

Dee

By mid June, I still had not heard from Richard. I tried not to think about him, but it was hard. I missed his friendship. I missed feeling loved and wanted. Even though he couldn't say it, I felt sure he loved me. I clung to the hope that he would call one day and want to get back together. I got up early every morning to check e-mail, in case he contacted me.

On Friday, June 11, 2004 Olga sent a great report and a note from Alesia completely in English. I figured Olga had translated it, but I still was happy to see it.

Yesterday's visit to Alesia was a good and, at the same time a sad one. I talked to the vice-principal and she complained of the poverty in the orphanage, it was very hard to listen to it, especially being in the know that our education and kids don't have any real care and attention from our government. I saw more and more familiar faces in the orphanage and noticed their poor and dirty clothes. Alesia told me they wash in the tub in the bathroom, they have very few clothes and toys (she has only 5 soft toys! Oh, My!), but she didn't complain, she only answered my questions and it seemed she even didn't really realize the other better life.

*When telling my Zoya [her daughter] about the poor environ-
ment in the orphanage I cried and saw she also felt very upset. We
decided to ask our students to collect some clothes, toys and other
things for the kids, and we will do our best for it. Our Lyceum helps
another orphanage next to our school (there are kids aged 2-6), give
them concerts, collect toys and books, and help to repair the building.
But Alesia's home is in the worse position, and I am very frustrated
with it. The vice-principal shared they were allowed to visit the circle
[the center of town] for free but they didn't have any money to rent
the bus and now she looks for the sponsor to pay the rent.*

*She has talked to the principal and he explained that first he
needed to talk to me, in a week he would come back from his business
trip, and I hope everything would be OK and the little one could celebrate two birthdays (Zoya's and hers) with my family.*

*When asking Alesia why she didn't draw a picture for mom
and granny I felt the girl being upset, it turned out she (and some
other girls) doesn't have any soft-tip pens and pencils. Poor, poor
things. And I wondered why she didn't color the pictures in the special
colored books I brought to her. She doesn't have anything to color and
paint with! I'll bring her Zoya's soft-tip pens "Crayola" but I will
appreciate if you put the new box of such soft-tip pens for Zoya into
the parcel as well.*

*Here is Alesia's letter to you. She is a smart girl and starts to
read and write some words and expressions.*

Take care, Olga.

With great excitement, I read Alesia's letter. It was short and
cheery. I was so happy to know that she prayed and that she
understood about God. It simply said:

Dear Mom Dee! Dear Granny Elva!

*I want to tell you why I thank Jesus every night that you're my
mom. I'm studying English. I like English.*

Kiss you! Alesia

A few days later I wrote in my journal,

Well, the grief over Richard has kind of sunk in and hurt more over the last few days—sort of a delayed reaction. So I am just sad, feeling very alone. I have felt angry at him, but also angry at myself for failing again. It's just a painful wound. I had so hoped he was the right guy for me. I feel such a sense of failure. I keep praying about it, and it helps, but doesn't alleviate all the pain...

A few days later, I got a great note from Olga. I wasn't surprised that once Olga saw Topolevo, she would try to help the kids:

On Wednesday I'll visit Alesia and ask her about the crayons. I also will bring some of Zoya's books (Alesia told me she likes to read) and toys as well. There is also a nice US dress small for Zoya but just of Alesia's size. I hope she would like it. (A lot of Zoya's clothes were given to our church and neighbors)

When talking to the vice–principal I wondered why the girls are watching TV so much (those dull serials) instead of creating something or planting some flowers, or taking care of any animals, and she answered that the tutors aren't interested in such work. Of course it's easier to sit on the sofa and watch TV with the children instead of playing games, reading books or creating something. I've read the summer plan on the wall and there was nothing interesting for the kids. They even don't do morning exercises. I wasn't happy to see some elder girls and boys smoking on the house's porch. I suggested the vice-principal to share "Hands and Words Are Not for Hurting" for all the children and she was happy with this idea. So, after Zoya's exams we'll go to the orphanage (maybe Olga—the student who visited Ann Kelly, the Purple Hands Project creator, in March 2003 with me—can join us as well). If you visit: **http://www.handsproject.org** *you can see some familiar faces.*

It was comforting to know that Olga was seeing Alesia every week and reaching out to the other kids there. It gave me a little brightness in an otherwise bleak time.

Chapter Thirteen

FRANTIC PRAYERS

The next day, another blow. I wrote in my journal:

Well, just when I thought things couldn't get worse, they now suck on a large scale. I am having problems at work. I also think layoffs are a distinct danger. I was told by my boss today that I will have to do something extraordinary if I want to keep my job—take on extra responsibilities, learn new skills, etc. I've heard it before, and my standard reply is that's fine, but I need training and some guidance. I don't think that's unreasonable.

Madeline was very curt in the meeting. She also let Peter sit in and, when I tried to tell her about the issues with him and get everything out in the open so we could discuss it, she wouldn't listen. She said I should have been learning new skills — by myself. She had always been supportive, but she had suddenly turned into a cold, mean person that I didn't know any more. I was left with the impression that she liked Peter, not me, and wanted me gone, for reasons that didn't really make any sense.

I didn't really want to quit, but the situation seemed hopeless. I came home and started sending out resumes. I couldn't even talk about it to anyone but Mom. I was very hurt. Madeline knew I was going through a very stressful time and, instead of being supportive, just heaped on more misery.

I tried to focus on papering Atlanta with resumes and praying a lot. I also tried to be mindful that, in the big scheme of my life, it wasn't the worst thing in the world. It was so hard to stay positive. I had always felt that, even though it wasn't really my passion, I was at least a competent paralegal. Madeline's criticism just made me feel like I had been betrayed by a friend.

For the next few weeks, every time I got in the car and had time to think, I cried. The three biggest things in my life—Richard's love, the job I had liked, the hope of getting Alesia home soon — were all gone or slipping away. It was overwhelming. I cried and cried, and prayed for strength.

One nice distraction during that terrible June was the preparation of Alesia's birthday box. Mom sent a box with several nice presents in it for her—tennis shoes, a sweatshirt, and a cosmetics bag with soap, a washcloth, etc.

A few days later, I was delighted to get another letter from Alesia, through Olga. Alesia was writing so well. I was thrilled with how well she was doing. Her letter was brief—she said:

Dear Mommy and Granny! Thank you for your love. I know many English words. (She then lists the English words she knew—a lot of nouns. No verbs.)

She also put down her little prayer she says:

Dear God, I love you so much. You have done so many great things for me. In Jesus name, Amen.

Love, Alesia

I was so glad she understood the importance of prayer. I decided that, one day when she became fluent in English, I would tell her about my dream and my belief that God put us together to be a family.

In the midst of all my troubles, I got a call that put things in perspective. My friend and cousin Jan Rusin called the next morning to say her father had passed away the previous night. There were many phone calls back and forth. I felt so bad for Jan. I remembered how desolate I had felt when my father died.

I sang at the funeral, which was held in the little town of Canton (north of Atlanta). The funeral was an ordeal (I was sad, remembering my father's funeral) but the singing went well and I felt like I did a decent job. I sang *Amazing Grace*, without accompaniment. I tried to put a lot of feeling into the song, which wasn't hard. I'd felt the amazing grace of God in my own life and I knew that power.

I had made a pound cake and, after the service took it up to the house of a relative where everyone gathered. I was complimented on the cake. It was comforting to remember I could do some things really well, like baking and singing. The adoption delays, the job situation and the breakup with Richard had been so depressing.

I had not forgotten about Alesia's birthday coming up in July. Once again, I drove up to Acworth so Kate could help with filling out the mailing forms. Mailing stuff to Russia is not fun. I got Alesia's birthday box mailed off, plus other boxes containing the gifts for Olga, Larissa, and Tamara. Kate and I really worked to get three boxes redistributed to five, since the three were too heavy.

I had put in five rolls of toilet paper and some old (but clean and usable) towels for the kids. I had noticed their towels looked woefully small when I was there in May.

I know that everyone in the small town Acworth post office thought Kate and I looked peculiar, squatting on the floor with all these boxes around us, frantically stuffing rolls of toilet paper and old towels in there amongst the games and toys and gifts. Kate's friend who worked there helped us. We were running against a deadline—the post office was closing soon. I worried that there might be problems with the declared value, but I told Kate that, if her aunt Tamara ended up having to pay customs taxes, I would reimburse her.

Kate filled out all the paperwork in Russian. We were both sweating when it was over. What a relief it was to get it done.

Sending off the boxes was something positive I could do to help Alesia, and it made me feel better. But I still needed R&R. I spent some time with my friend Maria that Saturday night. We saw a movie and went to dinner afterwards.

I told Maria about my job situation. She understood a lot, since she was also a paralegal. It helped me to express my thoughts to her. I decided to just tell Madeline on Monday that I would work out a notice and then leave. I knew if I tried to stay Peter would make me miserable, since he resented me so much, and Madeline wouldn't help me. I just worried about getting another paralegal job before returning to Russia.

The next Tuesday I had another meeting with Madeline and Peter. I told them I had decided to leave. Now it was their turn to look stunned. I admitted that I was already looking for another job.

I said, "As I see it, there are several options. I can stay until I find something else, or give two weeks notice, or I can clean out my cube now." The moment the words "clean out my cube now" were out of my mouth, they both shouted "No, no, don't clean out your cube now!" This was sort of funny. They had put me through so much hell that I had to admit I enjoyed watching them squirm.

So they agreed that I would work until I found something else. It was a relief, really, and by agreeing to that, I thought Madeline perhaps felt guilty about the way she acted. I was still pretty bitter about her behavior.

When I had had some time to reflect, I decided that I felt

relieved to be looking for another job. I was tired of the job I had, which had stopped being fun and started being nerve-wracking as soon as Peter had started. And I felt that they were being very unreasonable.

I had planned to look for another job after the adoption was complete and I had Alesia home. I felt that the company was very unstable. However, I really hated the anxiety of finding another job before I was called to go back to Russia—timing was crucial. I had to have a job when I went into the adoption hearing or they might not let me complete the adoption. I prayed all the time, every day.

Finally, on June 29, there was good news. Kate called and said all five boxes had arrived safely in Khabarovsk. Tamara had e-mailed Kate and said she would deliver them to the kids whenever she could get a ride to the orphanage. I was so relieved.

Although most people were very supportive about my adoption plans, some were negative.

My friend Margaret, who had initially been very supportive, told me on the phone that she was SURE that Alesia had FAS (Fetal Alcohol Syndrome). She said that practically all Russian orphans had FAS and/or were screwed up emotionally, that I would need all kinds of extra counseling and therapy for her, and that there was no way she would be normal. She made all these horrible statements based on ONE child she knew of who had been adopted from Russia. It was very unfair of her, I felt. She wouldn't listen to me when I told her she was wrong. I just resolved to not call her again, because I didn't need that negativity. I figured if she ever called me to apologize I would re-think it, but I wasn't going to hold my breath waiting for that call.

One of my cousins also told me I was crazy to adopt an older child—based on ONE adopted child he knew of from Russia who was a discipline problem. I argued with him, but he was sure I was wrong. He's basically a sweet person, so it was really shocking to hear him be so harsh.

My brother was also making gloomy predictions. He felt sure I was taking on too much. I knew these predictions were fear-based.

All these naysayers were daunting, but I was able to see past their negativity. I couldn't argue with them that my confidence and comfort came from faith—they wouldn't accept that. I felt sorry for them. I couldn't wait for them to meet Alesia and learn how wrong they were.

I continued to send out resumes and was called for interviews. I had a good resume and I had never had much trouble landing interviews in the past. I decided to be totally honest about the adoption. I wanted to take off at least a month of leave afterwards to make the adjustment to being a parent and get Alesia settled.

When I got home from one interview I had a great surprise—a note from Olga saying Alesia was going to visit her for the weekend. I sent this reply:

Oh Olga, I am so glad they are letting you take her for a visit! That's the best birthday present I could get! THANK YOU!!

Please give this to Alesia:

Dear Alesia -

I am so delighted to hear that you are spending some time with Olga and Zoya. You are a lucky girl. Please do whatever they ask you to do, and thank them for their kind hospitality.

I am going to spend the weekend with Granny Elva in Augusta. Sunday is my birthday. I will be 42 years old. Sunday is also the birthday of America—July 4 is Independence Day, celebrated since 1776 when we declared our independence from England. Some of my ancestors fought in the American Revolution.

Granny has a new puppy, a tiny little thing named Coco. The puppy is all black except for 4 white paws and a white chest. I will send a photo when I can. I bought Coco because Granny loves dogs, and her old dog died a few weeks ago. Coco is a house dog—she even sleeps with Granny. Perhaps when you go to Granny's house Coco will sleep with you, if you want. She is very clean, and will never be a big dog.

I wish I could be with you on your birthday, sweetheart, but I cannot. You are always in my thoughts and prayers, and I will bring you home as soon as I can.

The next day, on Friday, July 2, 2004, I got up and checked e-mail, and found a sweet note and drawing, sent by Olga, from Alesia:

Dear Mom!

I like to be at Olga Nikolaevna and Zoya. When I came in I started to explore the flat, there is very beautiful here.

How are you, Mommy? How is Granny? I am fine. The days are very hot, there are few rains.

I have drawn a picture to Zoya, she liked it very much. Then I watched English cartoons, they were very interesting. Then I helped in the kitchen. We bought food in the nearest store, and 17 red roses for Zoya's birthday at the market.

When I left for Olga's and said good bye to all the girls.

With big love, Alesia

I am not sure what she meant by the last sentence. Didn't

matter. I just thanked God she was able to be with a nice family and see what it was like. I sent her a reply:

> *What a great letter! Thanks so much, Sweetheart. Your*
> *drawing is beautiful. You are such a talented artist.*
> > *I am so glad you are having a nice time with Olga and Zoya.*
> *Tell Zoya I wish her a very happy birthday.*
> > *It is raining a lot here, every day. It isn't too hot, yet. We are all*
> *tired of the rain. The flowers and grass look nice and green, however.*
> > *Be a sweet girl and help Olga and Zoya.*
> > *Much Love,*
> > *Mom/Dee*

I left that Friday after work and drove to Augusta to spend the weekend with Mom. I could check e-mail there, too. Olga sent this:

> *Alesia is so excited to be with the family, she followed me*
> *everywhere like an alley cat, helped in the kitchen, (there was cheese*
> *and sausage and tea for lunch and Russian borsch, salad, and coffee*
> *with milk and cake for dinner), went shopping, watched Disney's*
> *cartoons (in English), played with Thomas [the cat] and toys, studied*
> *language with me, and was very happy. My kids were also very*
> *friendly with her. I washed her in the bathtub, and she asked me to*
> *allow her to watch cartoons before going to bed.*
> > *Today is Zoya's birthday, she turns 17, and all the family is*
> *excited with this special event of our baby. I've bought 17 beautiful*
> *red roses for her (Alesia helped me to choose them at the market), in*
> *the morning we gave Zoya nice gifts, and in the evening was a small*
> *family tea-party. We plan to go to the river bank for barbeque*
> *tomorrow to celebrate Zoya's birthday in the nature.*

How did you like Alesia's picture drawn for Zoya's birthday?
The words are: Happy Birthday, Zoya. Her letter was written by her
in Russian first and then we translated it together with the help of the
computer.

When I got up the next morning I had another e-mail from
Olga:

You are wonderful persons and Alesia is so lucky that God has
crossed your paths…
I think you will not have a lot of problems with Alesia's adapta-
tion, she is a kind sociable girl and attracts people to herself. I like
her asking me "Anything to help?"—it's the question I taught my own
children since the very early ages of their life and I am proud that
they are very helpful people. The same is your child. She is an
obedient girl as well and does everything she's asked to do. Here are
some written exercises she did when learning English today (two in
her copy-book and one with the computer help) and a new picture.
The task was to translate the sentences and correct some wrong. She
didn't talk much over the phone, you know, she isn't used to speak
over the phone, was a bit shy to talk with you, and her speaking
English is still poor.
Roman drove us to the nearest forest where we spent a very
nice time at the picnic among the blossoming shamrock and other
wild flowers. The birthday party was continued at home with a big
cake, tea, fruits, candies and ice-cream. I share the photos as soon as
they would be developed.
May God be with you, Olga (and the gang)

A little while later, I was delighted to get another update
from Olga, telling us more about the weekend:

Alesia was so tired and excited with·all the new things she experienced in my family that slept till 1pm today (she went to bed at 10.30 pm yesterday). We had lunch and our classes and now are ready to go to the city center (Alesia, Zoya and I) to have a bit of rest there and visit the jewelry store to buy earrings for Zoya (a gift from the relatives, you know). Then we'll take your girl to the orphanage.

I called Tamara, and she'll give Larisa your gift to Zoya and we'll take it later. Thank you very much.

During our lesson Alesia wrote a letter to you (with my help, of course; she has read it aloud several time) and include the birthday card as well. Here it is:

Dear Mom! Dear Granny!

Happy Birthday to you, Mommy Dee! I wish you happiness, health, and love. I dream to be with you. Happy Independence Day too!

Yesterday we had a picnic in the nature. We made a fire, prepared shashlyk (barbeque), lied in the sun, picked up flowers, and had a rest. I am very pleased to be in Olga's family.

Hugs and kisses, Alesia

It was so sweet of Olga to be so nice to Alesia. I winced when I read about them taking her back to the orphanage, though. Poor baby. I thought, now she will miss the family because she knows what a good family is like.

I had been depressed at the thought of a birthday without Richard, without my brother coming for a visit, and with no joy, really. The notes from Olga made it bearable. The real highlight of the weekend had been the phone call to Alesia.

I had to wait until 10:20 p.m. Friday, which was 1:20 Saturday afternoon their time, but it was great to hear Alesia's voice. I said "Hello, how are you?" and "I love you" in Russian. She said "I love you Mom!" in English. Olga had to translate the rest of the time. Alesia read a poem she had written (in Russian).

Mother also talked to her for a moment, then started crying and had to hand the phone back to me. She is not a person who cries often, but she was just overwhelmed with emotion.

Alesia has a deep, husky little voice. I had the same kind of voice as a child. Mom said that's what got to her.

I got home Sunday night, and Kate sent me a message that night saying that she had heard from Tamara and the presents were delivered to Alesia. I was happy she had some things from me to cheer her up, even though she was back at the orphanage.

As I tried to sleep that night, I just had to cry a bit. I missed Richard. I had sent him a couple of e-mails after the breakup call, and he had not responded. I had left him a voicemail—no response. So his statement that he wanted to be friends was not true. He didn't even send me an e-mail saying Happy Birthday. It was like he had dropped off the planet. I grieved. I tried to sleep.

I finally got out of bed. I took all of Richard's photos, notes and cards to me, tore them up, and threw them away. I was mentally and emotionally trying to let go, which was very painful. He had never sent back my things back that I left at his house. I was angry with him. His behavior had been dishonorable and rude, I felt.

I wrote in my journal, "I am well rid of him."

Despite those words, the pain of that breakup gripped my heart for a long time. It's hard to let go of a dream.

Chapter Fourteen

THE DOLDRUMS

In mid July, I got an e-mail from Masha saying to go ahead and complete the dossier documents and make my medical appointment. The medical test results had to be no more than three months old before I could go to court for the adoption hearing. Could I be hopeful that I would travel soon? I didn't know.

Finally, I decided to go home on my lunch hour a few days later and call Masha from home. Masha was very rude and yelled at me on the phone! It was bizarre. Masha made it clear she didn't like dealing with me because I asked too many questions. She accused me of not trusting her when I suggested I hire a private investigator to find the parents' marriage license and clear up the issue of the mom's name. I am a paralegal; that's how I think. It had nothing to do with not trusting. I also wanted to know when I might travel. She was really rude and refused to say. I explained I had every right to ask for information. She said other parents weren't so much trouble, the agency had never had an adoption fall through, etc. etc.

After we hung up, I was really angry. I was right—there was no progress on the adoption, but they wanted all the rest of the paperwork and more money—$7,000! (Months later, I heard from a number of other families that were very dismayed by their treatment by the agency. I am not using their real names here, for that reason.)

The next week was very difficult emotionally. The conversation with Masha was so upsetting. I thought about changing agencies. I didn't want to change agencies though, because it would be such a pain to start over.

I kept trying to come up with ways I could help the situation in Russia with the missing document verifying the birthmom's marriage, but nothing solid came to mind. I knew if I hired someone on my own, with Kate's help, it would really make Masha mad, too, and I thought, Lord knows what she might do. She had sounded pretty unstable mentally on the phone.

My biggest fear was that Masha might try to force me to give up on Alesia and adopt another child. She kept trying to persuade me to do that. However, I was far too attached to Alesia to do that. I couldn't bear the thought.

I sent an e-mail to Danny Griffin and told him about the situation. He had traveled to Russia for many years and knew the country very well. Danny suggested that, if I sent Masha the $7,000, the situation might be cleared up. He's pretty pragmatic, for a missionary. I sent the money and prayed.

I went to my Cousin Tony's wedding in Lexington the next weekend and that was a nice diversion. I was glad to get away and do something different. The drive up there is through the mountains and it's very pretty. It was also good to relax and visit with family and old friends.

I kept looking at all the little children at the wedding, though, and wishing they were mine.

The whole weekend, I kept seeing Toyota Avalons (Richard's car) everywhere, and other things that reminded me of Richard. Despite my efforts to move on, the grief got worse. I missed him terribly. I was still angry with him, but I just missed him, too. We had been close friends, had shared our lives for months. The sadness was still overwhelming at times.

I made an appointment with Dr. Bailey for my medical exam. It included a regular examination, plus tests for AIDS, syphilis, TB, etc. The doctor had to fill out forms. You have to be a healthy person to adopt from Russia.

The next day, I got an e-mail from Masha at the agency saying simply:

The letter from Vital statistics office arrive, Olesya's paperwork is cleared for the process.

I read it and re-read it several times. I was so relieved. All the heartache and emotional turmoil, and one short e-mail told me it was solved. It would take me some time to process that, emotionally.

Adoption events proceeded at a mad pace—start and stop, start and stop. Hope, despair, hope. I recited the 23rd Psalm all the time. I prayed constantly.

The next morning I wrote to Alesia:

Dear Alesia,

I hope you are having a good summer. It is very hot here and it rains a lot.

I got your letter from Olga that said you had been swimming. That's terrific. I love to swim. There is an outdoor pool here at the condo and when the weather is nice you can swim every day if you like. It's great exercise. When I was a kid I swam on a swim team for four summers. It was a lot of fun.

Granny's new puppy keeps her very busy. Her name is Coco, and she weighs less than 5 lbs. She is all black except her paws and belly are white. She likes to run around the house and play with little balls. She also likes to bite Granny's shoes, her hair, fingers, etc.—but not hard. Her teeth are coming in and that's why she wants to bite everything.

Keep studying English. You are doing wonderfully. The more you learn, the easier it will be when you come here. I am glad you like to learn the language. Granny and I will both help you to improve when you come over here, and the school will teach you, too.

I still don't know exactly when I can come and get you. There are some delays with the documents. It may be later this fall, maybe even November or December, before I can get there. I am praying every day about it. I know you are praying, too.

Even though I am not there with you, you are always in my thoughts and in my heart. I am so blessed to be getting such a wonderful daughter.

Much Love,
Mom Dee

By then end of July, things started looking up. I heard from Masha that I could use the employment verification from the home study in the final dossier package of documents to go to Russia, and not have to get a new one. I had misplaced it, but I finally found it. It was still true, since I was still employed at Garland Hotels at that time. I was so relieved to find that I could wait and give the court a new employment verification when I got the new job and went over for the hearing. I had been worried I'd have to find a new employer to sign a new verification form before I could send over the final batch of documents.

I spent a good bit of time sorting through the documents to see what I still needed to send and what I needed to do. I faxed a note to my doctor, too, telling her I now needed two copies of the medical. She was really nice about filling out the form—everyone in her office seemed to be pulling for me and went out of their way to be helpful.

The job search was frustrating. I had gone on several interviews. None of the jobs I interviewed for worked out. I renewed my efforts, and they paid off with three interviews in one week. None of them was my dream job, but at that point I just needed any job. I was worried.

The next day, I got up and had a great e-mail surprise—photos of Alesia, taken when she was at Olga's flat in July. She looked thin, but radiant. My favorite photo was of her holding Olga's large cat, Thomas. Her hair was down and looked lovely, and she looked delighted. It was the first time I had seen her hair clean, seen the cascade of gorgeous blonde curls.

On the last Friday in July, Olga sent an e-mail about registering her daughter for college, but didn't say a whole lot about Alesia. She included some new photos. One was of Alesia with Leonid, the orphanage director! That one was sort of startling. I decided that Alesia probably saw him every day, though, and he didn't intimidate her.

The following Sunday, August 1, 2004, I had a letter from Alesia that filled me with joy—just seeing the words "Dear Mama" were thrilling:

Dear Mama!

Our weather is very good. We were given two puppies: boys, they are very handsome. I go out often, play with the doggies and run with them across the field.

Olga Nikolaevna delivered some money given by her American friend to our orphanage, and Leonid Nikolaevich promised to buy school writing-materials for us.

I enjoyed the swimming pool very much; I have visited it 3 times. The other orphanage has been building behind our one and we plan to move there.

I've got your mail letter as well, thank you. Mama, I promise to pray for our meeting in the near future.

On August 3 or 4 we go to the camp, I have a great wish to go there.

Olga Nikolaevna gave me the photos from Zoya's birthday.

Kiss and love you and Granny! Alesia.

By August 5, I noted I got my last document apostilled and sent off the last [I hoped] package of adoption documents to the agency. The agency gave me information that it would probably mean I'd travel sometime in October. After the hearing, there was a 10 day waiting period for the adoption to be final. After the 10 days, we would have to stick around an extra day or two so Alesia could get a new birth certificate and passport. Then, a few days in Moscow and it would be time to travel home. There was a new level of excitement for me.

When I was driving home the next night, I kept seeing things and wondering how Alesia would see them. What will she think of the many flowers everywhere? Or the giant inflatable figures that businesses like to use to advertise—you never see those in Russia. Or Wafffle House—she's never eaten at one! It's not haute cuisine but I do love that place.

I was trying to stick to a low-carb diet, which was usually successful, but all the anxiety I felt over the job, the adoption, and the sadness over Richard just overwhelmed me. I couldn't stick to a healthy eating plan for more than a day or two. It was very frustrating.

By the middle of August, I had to note in my journal:

"A truly awful, discouraging day. A job I thought would work out, didn't. The recruiter called me this morning and they had an

offer for me. I told him to tell them I'd accept it, conditional upon them understanding about me missing 3-4 weeks due to the adoption. He called back late this afternoon saying they withdrew the offer, saying they have a big trial coming up and they can't let me miss that much work.

Now I have this dread fear I won't be able to find another job, and the whole adoption will fall through. It's a horrible catch 22—no job offers because of missing work for the adoption, and no adoption because I don't have a job. I don't know what I am going to do.

I am praying hard. I am trying not to lose hope.

I have cried most of the evening."

I am normally not a person who cries a lot. It seemed that I couldn't stop crying that night, however. I sat on the sofa and sobbed and sobbed. I was so afraid. I was so filled with anxiety. I worried that I would cry too loudly and my neighbors would call the cops. I cried into my arm when the sobs got too loud.

I kept thinking, "God don't let me fail. Don't let me fail. I must NOT fail Alesia. I must get her home, get her out of there. I must not fail. Please, please, please don't let me fail her." It was truly the lowest point of a very traumatic summer.

I spent some time with friends the following weekend, and made my friend Paul a birthday cake. Still, the sadness persisted.

As I've noted, the driving times were the worst. My commute was about thirty minutes each way to work. That's when nothing occupied my mind. That's when I missed Richard, worried about the adoption, and worried about the job search. As a person of faith, I felt somewhat guilty about worrying, but I couldn't help it. I did pray a lot, though.

For a while, I tried the Stevie Ray cure. While commuting,

I would put in a Stevie Ray Vaughn CD and try to "zone in" to the music and block out all other thoughts. His guitar playing was so complex and rich that it helped me a lot to concentrate on it and divert my thoughts from worry.

Finally, toward the end of August, I began to sense the end of the journey. On August 22, I wrote:

"Things are looking up, somewhat. I am feeling more optimistic, have been better able to stick to my diet, and the job situation seems promising. I went to Maria's last night for dinner, and she gave me a lot of little toys that she and another mother had found which their boys don't play with, or which were party favors (little cowboys/Indians, little books, etc.) and I can give those to Svitlana to give to the boys at the orphanage.

I have a second interview at a firm tomorrow, and a second interview at Home Depot on Tuesday. Surely one of those will result in a job offer."

Late that night, unable to sleep, I decided to play the game where you flip open the Bible at random and see where your finger lands. I thought it was pretty prophetic that this is where it landed:

"It is God that girdeth me with strength, and maketh my way perfect."

Psalm 18:32

I believe in signs. I felt this was a sign that I was going to get through the difficult transition and come out okay. I went to bed that night feeling very relieved.

Chapter Fifteen

THE TIDE TURNS

On Saturday, August 28, I wrote in my journal, with great elation:

"Yesterday I got a job offer from Home Depot. Yay! Finally a real offer. I had to go take a drug test (pee in the cup), and they are running a background check, but once that's done, it's a real offer. I spoke to the HR guy before they sent the offer package, and asked him to make sure with the attorneys that they would let me have time off for the adoption, and provide me with an employment verification, and he called back and said they were fine with it. What a huge relief."

I knew the adoption had been the reason why I had not gotten jobs. I had interviewed with several firms where I had friends and, of course, they knew about the adoption. Most law firms won't choose a paralegal who, almost immediately, has to take several weeks off. One of my friends even suggested I postpone the adoption until I got my job situation straightened out. I knew I couldn't do that. It would just cause me so much grief. The worry over the job situation had been so nerve-wracking, though. Every time I started to panic, I just prayed, God please let it all work out.

The Home Depot folks were obviously different. Home Depot prides itself on being a family-oriented company, and it is true. If one needs time off for family reasons, it's usually given. Employees work hard, but by and large are treated fairly.

I was also pleased to go to work for a place where I could do employment law. I had done a very limited amount of it at the hotel company, and was never allowed to manage cases. At Home Depot, I was told I'd be responsible for managing 30-40 cases and would not have to handle any more hotel "slip and fall" cases. (Those are cases where someone slips, gets hurt, and sues the property owners.) I have always been fascinated by employment cases involving racial discrimination, sexual harassment, gender discrimination, etc.

So a huge weight was lifted, knowing my job situation was going to be OK.

I finally heard from Olga that she had been to see Alesia and had sent a note from her. Olga had been out of town. It was so good to hear from her:

My visit to the orphanage was successful today: Alesia was very glad to see me and have English lessons again; she loved beautiful angels I brought from China for her and Nadia. (By the way, I also collect angels; we have so much in common, Dee) I have visited Alesia's school today and talked to the vice-principal: she agreed to allow Alesia to study English instead of German at school. Of course it would be hard for your girl, but I promise to help her as much as possible.

The orphanage's vice-principal showed me the stationery they've bought for the kids with the money sent by my friend from Montana, I've taken the photo of that stuff as well as the photo of Alesia, Nadia and Olia with the orphanage dogs, I'll send it to you after developing.

I attach Alesia's letter written in both languages, and the translation of it as well. It's not very neat and has some mistakes, but it was written from her heart while looking at the cards of Atlanta and the small guardian angel in red dress.

Alesia wrote:

Dear Mom and Grand Mom!
I am happy to be in the orphanage (she meant to come back from the camp). *I was in the camp "Gull". I don't* (didn't) *love it very much. We greeted the dawn, swung at the swing, and had a disco. We were full-fed.*
We didn't bathe in the river, because the Amur water is dirty. We had light athletic, exercises and games.
I and Nadia have angels. They are from Olga and Zoya.
I will study English at school.
I love and miss you.
Kiss you. Alesia.

Mom and I laughed over the phrase "we were full-fed." Obviously she wasn't fed to the point of being full too often at the orphanage. She was very thin in the photos. I was a little concerned as to why she didn't like camp, but I figured she was just restless and wanted to be adopted. As hard as the waiting was on me, I knew it had to be much tougher for her.

I had a strange piece of news on August 31—the director of the orphanage had suddenly died. Olga sent an e-mail. I opened it early that morning:

I have some good and bad news to share with you. And I start with the bad one asking you to pray for the orphanage principal Leonid who has died this morning from leucaemia. Nobody expected this, yesterday he celebrated his 46 birthday. I've seen him just before my trip to China while giving him donation from my Montana friend. It's good that I've taken the photos of Alesia with him, I think. He was a remarkable person. He did all his best to take care of the poor orphanage kids, he complained to me how tired he was with all the problems, how hard it was to explain the orphanage needs to the bureaucrats, and now the result of many life's aspects and the hard work as well.

The good news is that there I met Danny Griffin, the kids were hanging on him like grapes. He, Patrick and Svetlana brought some gifts to the children and were ready to entertain them, but instead they prayed and talked with kids how short our life is and how careful we need to be to each other. Danny will leave on Sept 3 and I hope to give a small gift to you as well as Alesia's pictures via him. The photo of him, I, Alesia, Nadia and other kids were taken to show to you.

Very odd—the director was only 46. I felt sorry for the children, many of whom had been there for years. He was their only father figure. What a blessing Danny and Svitlana were there and could do immediate grief counseling.

For selfish reasons, of course, I hoped his death wouldn't negatively impact the adoption. I had a brief moment of panic about that. Had he signed all the papers? Would there need to be new signatures obtained? I e-mailed my agency about it. They checked on it and said he had signed off on everything before he died.

Alesia sent the following note, through Olga:

Dear Mom and Granny!

It's a sad day today. Leonid Nikolaevisch is dead.

Danny is here with gifts for kids: a pen, a pencil, a sharpener, a rubber, copy-books, and apple and an orange in a bag. Tomorrow is September 1. I want to go to school. I love school.

Love you, Alesia

I was very glad to hear she loved school. I hoped it was not just because she wanted to get away from the orphanage. She would be so challenged to function in the US and try to learn English quickly, I felt. I hoped that when she got to the US she would still say that she "loves school." I never loved school—I tolerated it. But I was a fat kid and got teased a lot.

On Friday, September 3, 2004, I watched with horror the situation in a Russian town where schoolchildren were kidnapped by Chechen rebels. The children were held for three days with no food or water. One of the news reporters caught a photo of a big Russian soldier looking like he was about to cry—how could anyone see those children covered in blood and not be sorrowful? It was so scary to me. Every time I saw those children I thought of Alesia. I couldn't help but write in my journal, "Thank God Alesia is far away from that."

The first weekend in September was spent with Mom in Augusta. We went to Target and got Alesia some clothes for traveling. We found a couple of pairs of sweatpants and several shirts, plus panties and socks. I decided I would pick up more things when it got closer to travel time. We couldn't find her a nightgown—all the kids were wearing PJ's now, apparently.

We went to a fabric store and found several lengths of pretty fabric to take to Olga as a gift from Mom. Olga and her daughter Zoya sewed a lot and I knew they would be able to make several nice outfits.

Preparations for the trip took up a lot of time. I had a chance to look at the handheld computer translation device I had ordered. It looked good for translating words back and forth, and Alesia could type in Russian, but sentences looked tricky. It had pre-programmed travel-type sentences, but I could not type in a sentence and get it translated. I decided it would work for what I needed it for, though. It also said the words, but the sound quality of the voice was poor. I figured Alesia would be more intrigued by it than by a simple Russian/English dictionary.

I was thinking about traveling with Alesia, and what I might need to take in case she had an upset stomach or air sickness. I sent out an e-mail to friends and family members who had kids. I got some good advice from my cousins Linda and Terri and my friends Cissy, Joanne, and Kim. I also asked about where to find cute kids' clothes that weren't too expensive—the consensus was Gap Kids and Old Navy. I went online and looked at some of their clothes. It looked like the 1970's all over again. Thank God there is a uniform policy at her school, I thought.

Despite all the preparation, the paperwork, the adoption books I had read, and money I had paid, I had to admit that the whole adoption still seemed somewhat unreal. The actual idea of Alesia being my daughter still seemed like a far-away occurrence. A part of my brain just said Oh, no need to worry about the day-to-day mommy stuff until it happens. That will be a joyful challenge.

I tried to make myself listen to the Russian language CD's in the car but I was too antsy to listen and concentrate. I couldn't seem to get myself settled down at all. I had grown weary of reading parenting and adoption books. I settled in to re-read a favorite adventure book that was over 800 pages long. It helped to get my mind off the adoption wait.

Finally, on September 9, I had a reason to be cautiously optimistic. I heard from Masha that she had sent off the revised financial form and that the dossier would be filed in court within the week. I was elated.

Finally, it was time to start the new job. The summer had

been such an ordeal, job-wise. I was a lame duck at Garland Hotels. The lawyers had stopped giving me much to do. The lawyers rarely ever spoke to me, even to be civil. My co-workers were supportive about the adoption, but they had their own concerns.

The atmosphere was toxic—everyone feared more layoffs, and the lawyers gossiped incessantly about any paralegal that so much as spent two minutes talking to someone in the break room. There was a lot of suspicion and negative energy all around. I hated being there.

I was so ready for a change.

Chapter Sixteen

COUNTDOWN TO HOMECOMING

I took off several days between jobs. I had thought I would use the time to get some things accomplished around home and do some writing, but that didn't happen. I spent time just sitting and listening to the lashing torrential rains and rattling 50 mph winds from Hurricane Ivan.

When I was off work, I realized that it suddenly felt wrong to be alone. I had always been okay with being alone—I had lived alone for nearly twenty years. Suddenly, however, I missed Alesia. The condo felt very empty. Even talking to friends and Mom on the phone didn't help. Socializing didn't help. Nothing helped. I just prayed I would hear about the court date soon.

Preparations for bringing Alesia home continued. On September 18, 2004, Mom sent (at my request) some beautiful lace curtains for the windows in my living room. I hung them carefully. They really dressed up the room. In Russia, white lace curtains are everywhere. I hoped they would also remind Alesia a little bit of Russia, and help her feel comfortable.

My friend Maria and I wandered around a mall the next afternoon while her son roller-bladed at the skate park inside the mall. There were some good sales. I got Alesia a really cute pair of pajamas, pink with kitties on them, plus two dressy long-sleeved shirts. We found a great early season sale on coats and I got her an insulated, lined ski jacket in baby blue, marked down from $130 to $70. I felt very mom-like, buying clothes for my daughter.

On Monday, September 20, 2004, I started at Home Depot. I was in orientation all day in a training room—very boring. I wanted to say, just give me my apron and the manuals and turn me loose. At lunchtime, I went up to my department and said hello to some of my co-workers. Everyone was polite and friendly and wanted to know about the adoption.

My trip preparations continued. I went to Borders on my lunch hour of my second day at Home Depot and found four beautiful calendars with terrific color photos of nature scenes. I decided I would take those for gifts to Russia to the orphanage staff. They would be easy to pack.

I had worried about electrical outlets in Russia, and spent a lot of time trying to find the right adaptor/converter to take. I talked to Kate's husband, Bob, who knew all about Russian electrical current, having lived and worked there for a couple of years as a communications specialist. I finally got the electrical adaptor and step down converter in the mail that I had ordered. I was vastly relieved to have those. A lot of adaptors say they will fit Russian plugs, but they don't. I had worried about Ricky being able to recharge the cameras.

A few days later, I got some interesting news from Olga. I had wondered how Alesia did in school:

Dear Dee and Elva!
I would love you to be in the know of Alesia's school marks.
Here they are:
Algebra: 3 (4.09), 3 (8.09), 2 (14.09)
Russian: 3 (7.09), 2 (8.09), 4 (14.09), 3 (15.09), 3/4 (17.09)
Music: 5 (8.09)
Physical Training: 5 (16.09), 5 (18.09), 4 (23.09)
Physics: 5 (16/09)
Geography: 2 (18.09)
You know 5=A; 4=B; 3=C; 2=D
She visited one or two English classes at school (she didn't

remember exactly how many), but forgot to write down the home
task. So I wrote the message to the English teacher in her diary
asking her to take control of the girl.

> *She also didn't prepare the task given by me, since has lost the*
> *copy-book. And no letters and pictures for you, she explained that*
> *has forgotten.*

> *Alesia also didn't learn the prayer I translated for her, since it*
> *was in her lost copy book, and the computer class where I saved her*
> *papers in one computer's file was closed.*

> *So, such is news.*

> *Take care, deer Ladies, and may God help you with your*
> *generous but very hard mission.*

Alesia was stressed out, and, I was sure, missing Snezhana
already, knowing they would be separated soon. Mom sent Olga
an e-mail:

> *Thank you for Alesia's grades. I feel that the girl is showing the*
> *stress of waiting to be adopted and perhaps she feels discouraged and*
> *sad. When you see or talk to Alesia, please tell her to be brave a little*
> *longer. We love her very much. I was delighted that her music grade*
> *was good since Dee and I love music. I will teach her to play my*
> *piano.*

> *Olga, you are a truly wonderful person and so dear to our*
> *family! I am very grateful that we are friends! Take care.*

> *Love,*
> *Elva*

On Tuesday, October 5, 2004 I got an e-mail from Pasha,
my young friend in Khabarovsk. Pasha said he had been out to the
orphanage and had seen Alesia. He was being paid by a charity to

go out to the orphanage and teach the children computer skills, which I thought was terrific. I so hoped Alesia would pay attention and learn. I also hoped he would inspire her to study English. He taught himself English and is fluent in several other languages.

Another girl in Alesia's group, Snezhana, was being adopted, I had learned. Pasha met Snezhana's adoptive mother. He got her name and phone number for me, which I thought was awesome. I decided to call her when she got home from Russia.

On Sunday, October 10 I got a positive e-mail from Olga about Alesia's school work. She only said, however:

Alesia was praised for her good reading by the English teacher, good for her.

Olga also met Snezhana's mother:

Just a brief message to send you the email of Patti. I met her in the orphanage that Wednesday, a lovely lady. Snezhana and she were so happy to be together. Just after our conversation they went to purchase the flight tickets. I think she will tell you more about the adoption hearing when you contact you via email. She would be very glad to communicate with you.

Despite the positive developments, the waiting was starting to really get to me. It was very frustrating, waiting for a court date. I went to Mom's over the weekend and stayed busy, helping her clean out some things, running errands, and playing with the new puppy.

The day before I left I was playing the piano, and I started playing a song from *The Wiz* that I've always loved, called *Be A Lion*. It's about courage. I just started crying. All I could think about was how much I wanted to bring my little girl home, and how sad it was to go in her room and see everything and know she was so far away. I thought, I can't hold her or see her or anything yet.

Mom heard me and came in the room. She hugged me and told me to keep the faith and keep praying. I just keep praying, I told her. All the time. If it weren't for my faith in God's plan, I would be lost.

On Friday, October 15, finally, I got a break. Masha e-mailed and said the adoption hearing would likely be in early December. Yay! I called Ricky and told him the good news. I called Mom and told her the news. All day, the words "home for Christmas" echoed in my head. For the first time in many years, my mother's house would have a child in it—what a great day! That's what Christmas is all about—family.

I read a wonderful post on one of the Yahoo adoption message boards, written by a lady who adopted a little eleven year-old girl. They had birthday presents and a small party for the child. The little girl had never had presents or a party before—she told her mother nobody had ever said the words Happy Birthday to her! I cried when I read that, but I was so glad she posted it.

I decided to send Alesia a note:

Dear Alesia:

I have good news. The adoption agency says the adoption hearing will probably happen in early December. I don't know the exact date yet. I will come see you after the hearing, then return here. About ten days later I will return to Khabarovsk to get you. We should be home around Christmas. Here we celebrate it December 25.

I'm so sorry I could not make the adoption happen sooner. I have no control over the situation—only the court in Khabarovsk can decide when adoptions happen, sweeetheart. If it were my decision I would come get you tomorrow.

The good thing about you coming here in December, however, is that you will likely get here during the school holidays. Schools here close for two weeks, between December 20 and January 4, for Christmas. So when you get here you will probably have some time off to relax and get used to America before you must start school.

I know you are happy that Snezhana has been adopted, but sad because you miss her friendship. You are probably angry and frustrated, too, that I can't come and get you for another couple of months. Please try to be a good girl, however.

I miss you very much, but I pray for you every day. I love you more than anything in this world. Granny prays for you, too, and we look forward to bringing you home so much! She has many fun things planned for you to do. Christmas is Granny's favorite holiday.

Be a good girl, and do what Olga asks. I will write more details about the adoption when I learn more.

Love,
Mom

I told Olga I would let her know the exact court date as soon as I knew it. I hoped to hear something in the next few days.

Sunday, October 17, 2004, was a bittersweet day. I went to the Scottish Highland Games at Stone Mountain Park, which was usually a lot of fun. I just kept wishing Alesia was with us. I went with a group of my Henderson cousins every year. I tried to keep my spirits up and told my cousins that maybe it would be better for her to go the following year, when I could explain in English why there were a lot of men running around in kilts, and why bagpipes are important to people of Scottish descent…

Mom sent Alesia a letter, and I figured Olga would have a

tough time translating it, since it sounded exactly the way Mother talks:

> *Dear My Precious Most Absolutely Beautiful Alesia,*
> *How are you? Is it very cold there yet? When does it start to snow and ice? How do you keep warm? It is not very cold here, in Augusta, Georgia, and I do not know these things about Russia. When you come to us, we could write letters to your school in Russia and share information. I am just so very sorry that you are still not with us. However, it is not so long now, maybe mid-December. I prayed for you, your Mom Dee, and me at church, this morning. I pray for all of us every day and I KNOW my prayers are answered!*
> *We believe you will arrive around Christmas and that is a wonderful, happy time. I will help you and we will find Christmas presents for you to give your Mother and Uncle Bruce. Also, you can call your friend, who was recently adopted, and we will invite her and her Mom to visit soon. I love you so much and know we will meet soon. Be patient My Beautiful Alesia,*
> *Granny*

I kept reading on the message boards about other families getting court dates to adopt their kids. It was depressing. Finally, I had great e-mailed letters from Alesia and Olga:

> *Dear Dee and Elva!*
> *I was pleased with Alesia today; she did her home task well and was in good mood. This afternoon the girls said goodbye to Snezhana, tomorrow they leave for Moscow. Snezhana and Patty are so happy to be together. She told me she was glad to get your email, Dee.*
> *Dear Mom!*
> *I wish you to come so very much and wait for you all the time.*

It turns colder in Khabarovsk, and I want the winter to come sooner to play snowballs, to roll in the snow, to slide down the hills, to run on the snow and to have the New Year.

My favorite subjects are Physical Training, history, Computer class, Art, Craft and English.

Olga Nikolaevna told me the delightful news that you'll come to me in December. I am so happy to see you again and then celebrate Christmas and the New Year with you and granny. I still couldn't believe in this happiness.

I am so happy about Snezhana's good luck, tomorrow she and her mom fly to Moscow to get her visa and then to America. I will miss her.

I can read and translate English and know many words but it's still hard for me to speak. I think that in America I will learn it better.

I learn to make "a wheel" when there is nobody in the room.

With love, Alesia

I decided "make a wheel" meant to turn cartwheels. That's what Mom and I thought, anyway. I had to smile when I read that. I had loved doing cartwheels when I was Alesia's age.

By Saturday, October 30, 2004, I was praying and praying, and going nuts. I started to really worry that perhaps they would turn down the adoption for some reason, that I had done some of the paperwork wrong, or they thought I don't make enough money, or who knows. My imagination ran wild.

I met my friend Dana for a movie that day and we saw the new movie *Ray*—about Ray Charles' life. It was an excellent movie, though very sad in places. I found myself crying every time I saw a scene of him in childhood with his mother. I didn't cry loudly. I just couldn't help being weepy. It was very embarrassing.

I got an e-mail from Olga the next Thursday with two cute drawings attached, done by Alesia of course. One was a drawing of me. It looked nothing like me, but it was well done. The message from Olga was cryptic, but happy:

I had some minutes this morning to scan Alesia's pictures and composition. I was really surprised yesterday with her picture of Mom and a 5 in English she was so pleased to show me in her school diary.

Alesia's attached letter/composition was pretty funny. It looked like an exercise in writing English, but I'm not sure. Here is what she said:

My name is Alesia. I am in the seventh grade. I like dogs. I dislike peaches. My eyes are green. My hair is fair. I am tall and thin. My Mom's name is Dee. She lives in Atlanta. My granny's name is Elva. She lives in America too. I like to wear sports clothes. I have many hobbies: watching TV, reading books, and walking.

She sounded upbeat and optimistic. Mom and I thought the juxtaposition of the sentences about dogs and peaches was funny. My uncle remarked that once she tasted a good, ripe South Carolina peach, she would love peaches.

Later, that Sunday afternoon, I brightened up a lot. I spoke to Patti, the single mom that had adopted Alesia's best friend, Snezhana. Patti was really nice, very down to earth and easy to talk to.

Patti had met Snezhana in August of 2003 when she went over on a mission project with The Boaz Project. They do mission work in orphanages all over Russia. Patty is a nurse practitioner.

Snezhana had just been home a week. Patti said Snezhana had been sick and they didn't get to do any sightseeing in Moscow, but she was fine. Patty had the luxury of being able to stay home and homeschool Snezhana for the first couple of months and work with her intensely to learn English. She said Snezhana's English was coming along, but she still needed a lot of help.

I was still anxious to hear about the court date, but I was encouraged to hear that Snezhana was adapting well. I decided to help her and Alesia keep in touch, at least with phone calls, even if they could only see each other occasionally.

Talking to Patty helped me a lot. We didn't finish the conversation, though we talked for an hour. Just knowing that she had Snezhana and things were going fine was a real inspiration, and it gave me hope. Patty had never had biological children either. We were all learning to be mothers and daughters...

Chapter Seventeen

A RUSSIAN ADOPTION HEARING

Monday night, November 2. I was sitting on the sofa, in my bathrobe, idly channel surfing, when the phone rang.

Masha didn't waste time with pleasantries, but immediately said the court hearing was November 15! I was stunned. She apologized for not notifying me sooner, saying the hearing notice had gotten buried under something else. I barely heard her, I was so excited. Finally, I was going to get my girl!

I started making calls. I called Mom and she started laughing and crying at the same time. Mom said she had prayed ALL DAY that I would learn the court date today, and the Lord was listening!! I confessed to her I had been really depressed about the lack of news.

I sent out a delighted e-mail to all my friends and family.

It was hard to concentrate at work the next day. I called the travel agent at lunch. I went to Ricky's house after work to fill out the visa application for him. My mind was whirling with travel thoughts.

It was election day, but for the first time in my life I completely forgot to vote. It didn't even occur to me until late that night as I was falling asleep.

The next few days were very hectic, and I felt I was just hanging on for the ride. There were so many things to do and plans to make. I got my tickets and arrangements made. I had to leave Wednesday afternoon to get there by Friday morning. The agency had insisted I be there Friday morning, saying I had to be interviewed again by the Ministry of Education representative.

The next day, Olga sent this, from Alesia:

Dear Mom and Granny!
I love you very very much. We have vacation now. I wish
November Fifteenth come sooner to embrace and kiss you. We have
the dog Berta, she gave birth to two puppies (girls). One puppy is fat
the other one is thin. The fat one is brown and the thin cub is grey.
They are so funny, and like to play with each other. We built the dog
house for them, and made it habitable in winter. I am so happy that
you will take me from here forever. They are building some more
orphanages behind our ones to the other kids to live.
   With great love, Alesia

   I was so glad to hear she had told Alesia. I had written to
Olga about the travel plans and court hearing, then didn't hear
from her for a couple of days.

   I made more lists. I made lists of things to do (clean out
fridge, plan jewelry for court, copy passport and visa for luggage,
etc.), work to be completed, preparations for being gone (stop
mail, turn off heat, etc.). My purse overflowed with lists. I was
busy, but it was wonderful to finally be seeing the light at the end
of the tunnel.

   The next Monday was a harrowing day. I got almost eight
hours sleep the night before, which was highly unusual, but I was
really tired. I woke up that morning with no voice. Total laryngitis.
I took vitamins and drank gallons of water all day. Work was so
busy, trying to get things wrapped up. I worked from 8:00 until
6:00 without a break, except ten minutes to eat lunch.

   Just when my life seemed to be back on track—new job,
adoption plans becoming a reality—another bump in the road.

   The bank account situation was dire. I was out of ready

cash. I pondered getting a cash advance on my credit card. I hated that thought.

I got help from an unexpected source. My brother owed Mother some money—he had borrowed it when he got divorced. When he tried to pay Mother back, she told him to give me half of it to help with my adoption expenses. I'm sure he was taken aback by that.

Mom called me and told me about the money. The same day, he e-mailed and asked me for my Wachovia account number, since he banks there too. I was shocked that he would give me the money. I thanked him, and mentioned that the adoption expenses really had me stretched thin financially.

The next day he sent me an e-mail saying he had deposited $5,000 in my account—a gift, not a loan. I broke down in tears when I got home and read that.

I thought, my brother can be a real grump on occasion, but he comes through when I need him. I was still way in debt, but the money prevented me from having to go further in debt. I decided his heart had likely changed because he was starting to see that the adoption would actually be a reality.

Now, I thought, if God will just answer my prayer to give me my voice back.

The next Wednesday, November 10, 2004, was travel day. Ricky was not with me, because I had to make two trips. The first trip would be for the court hearing, then I had to fly home during the 10 day finalization period. I would go back and get Alesia and take Ricky with me then. I hated doing it that way but there was no choice. I couldn't miss so much work, when I had just started and had no leave time built up.

By 4:30 p.m. that Wednesday, I was in Chicago, waiting to

board the Swissair flight to Zurich. The Chicago airport was huge and confusing. I got there and discovered, after having to ask several people because there are no signs, I had to go to another terminal. I finally found the train to take me there. I was sweating, anxious, and exhausted by the time I found the gate for my flight. The flight to Zurich was uneventful, thank goodness.

In Zurich, we only had a little time between flights. I got off the plane and went in search of a store to buy bottled water. My throat was raw, from the long flight. I found a small storefront and some water, and noticed that time was running short. I put down my coat, paid in American money, grabbed my water and my backpack and took off running back to the plane. As soon as I got onboard and saw a man stowing a heavy coat in the overhead compartment, my heart sank. I had left my coat somewhere— probably in the little store.

The flight attendant was sympathetic, but wouldn't hold the plane so I could run back and get my coat. All I could do was fill out a form about the lost coat; they would try to locate it. I tried not to get too anxious about it. I would just have to buy a new coat, I decided.

When I got to Moscow, it was Thursday. I had a lot of anxiety. It took forever to find the right gate and get my boarding pass for the domestic flight to Khabarovsk. I had to ask a lady at the information desk, who explained to me in Russian how to find the Dalavia desk. Thank God I had studied Russian airport words. Then I stood in line forty minutes waiting to get a boarding pass. Then I had to go to another desk and pay extra for the overweight bags. The surly clerk wouldn't take a credit card, so I had to go get dollars changed to rubles and pay cash—about $30.

I was going to call Anatoly (the agency's Moscow person) and tell him about the coat situation, but I saw no pay phones anywhere. Good thing I didn't push for it—the 6:15 flight started boarding at 5:00.

I was at the actual gate freezing, standing next to an open door with big gusts of wind flying in. The baggage claim ticket flew out of my hand and landed somewhere under a big heavy desk. I dropped down to the floor, frantically searching. Everyone looked at me like I was nuts. I tried to explain about needing it— the Russians really check the claim checks against the bags you get when you arrive. One clerk was rude, another was nice. They gave me assurances I would be able to get my suitcase in Khabarovsk.

I thought, first I lose my coat, now I lose my baggage ticket. Yikes. This is not going well.

I walked down to the plane, freezing and worried. Completely exhausted, I settled in a bulkhead seat, right behind the world's stinkiest bathroom. After the plane took off, I was the third person in there and it already stank!

On Friday morning I got to Khabarovsk after flying all night, but nobody was there to meet me. You can park in front of the airport like you would park at a shopping center, and it's only 15 minutes from town. I was really ticked off. Finally, when I was starting to panic, Marina showed up. The agency obviously didn't care if she was late. She was wearing a tiny miniskirt, black leather boots, and a short coat. I know she was freezing. It was horribly cold and windy. She handled the problem with the lost claim check and I got both bags.

Thank goodness, parking at the Khabarovsk airport was not too far away. Walking across the icy parking lot with both my bags was brutal. My throat was so dry that it was on fire.

After killing myself to get to Khabarovsk to see the ministry of education lady Friday morning, I learned that I actually didn't need to see the Ministry of Education lady again. I had flown all the way over early for nothing!! I was so upset that I wanted to scream. I had taken extra days off work, paid top dollar for plane tickets, and was spending two extra nights in a hotel—just because I was told I HAD to get there by Friday morning. Aaaargh!

After checking into the hotel—the Intourist this time—I had time to just get a shower—thanks be to God—when Pasha called from the lobby. I was able to put on clean clothes. Traveling always makes me feel yucky.

I was glad to be in the Intourist, rather than the other hotel. It's big and drab, but there are several restaurants in the building, and I could exchange money at a booth in the lobby. There were also several gift shops.

I went downstairs feeling somewhat refreshed. It was great to see Pasha. He had a nice smile and he gave me a hug. We had a lovely lunch downstairs. He was worried about my being sick. I assured him that it was just laryngitis and a sore throat. The hot borscht in the hotel restaurant tasted so good.

After lunch, I went across the street to an upscale sporting goods store, but they only had one coat in my size and it was over $100. It was ugly, too. I was very glad I could make a choice not to buy it. Luckily, I had packed a heavy fleece shirt at the last moment. That, plus another shirt and long underwear was pretty warm if I just dashed from the building to the car. I also had a hat, scarf, and gloves.

Marina picked me up in the afternoon at the hotel. She was worried about my not having a coat. On the way to the orphanage, we stopped at a store. I tried on a coat that was sort of a brown quilted mandarin short jacket—not very warm. The department store looked more like a flea market with tiny booths of clothes, some of which were secondhand-looking and really gaudy. I decided against the brown coat since my fleece was warmer.

When we got to the orphanage, Alesia ran out to the car and gave me a big hug. Alesia looked wonderful, just still too thin. We weren't able to stay long—about an hour. I was informed that that was all the time possible. I wanted to shout, I just flew halfway around the world, and all I get is one lousy hour with Alesia?! I was so frustrated.

I talked to Alesia, with Marina interpreting. I stupidly asked her if she liked to go shopping, and she said she had never been shopping. I felt like an idiot. I told her all girls in America like to shop. I didn't mention that I hate shopping—most women look at me like I'm an escaped lunatic when I say that.

I also asked Alesia if she liked sports. She was not enthusiastic about any sport I mentioned. I asked her if she liked soccer and got a big reaction, "Football? That's for boys!" Alesia said she would like to try gymnastics, maybe swimming.

When I got back to the hotel, I was too tired to eat downstairs. I tried to order some pilmeni from the restaurant downstairs and they hung up on me. I had no idea how to say "room service" in Russian. I finally just ate a protein bar I had brought and went to bed.

I was so glad I had brought a pillowcase and sheet from home. The bed was rock hard—a mattress on a platform, like in college. It didn't matter—at least I could be horizontal. I slept like a dead woman. I was so tired. I had not been able to sleep much on the plane rides.

The next morning, breakfast was tasty. I could choose one of three breakfasts—a fairly normal American breakfast or a Russian breakfast with yogurt and cold vegetables. I chose American. I got a bowl of cornflakes, some cheese, bread, an omelet of powdered eggs, orange juice, and coffee.

When I got back from breakfast at 8:45, I tried to go to the business center and send an e-mail, but the business center was closed. Very frustrating.

I puttered around the room all morning and tried to rest.

For lunch, I got a hotel van to take me over to the Mar Kuel hotel, where I ate lunch with Jack and Dana, fellow adoptive parents I had met on a message board. Their apartment was very cozy. It had a full kitchen. We ate delivered pizza which tasted frozen, but it was fine. They were a nice couple. I felt so bad about their baby—she was in the hospital. They had only been allowed to visit her once, for a few minutes; another example of the agency's insensitivity.

Anya picked me up at the hotel at 2:30 and we went to the orphanage. I was able to spend some time with Alesia, just chatting, before the court prep. Anya and I spoke to the orphanage social worker, mainly about how I would take care of Alesia, my job change, etc.

Anya spent some time prepping Alesia for court, telling her how to act, what to say, etc. We were in the little schoolroom attached to the cloakroom in the orphanage. Kids wanted to come in and out and it was hard to keep them out.

Anya spoke Russian very fast. I asked her to repeat for me in English what she was telling Alesia and she snapped, "I will talk to YOU in a minute." I was startled. I felt like I had a right to know what she was saying to my child.

Anya also prepped me and it was about what I expected. She did say the agency asked the court to change Alesia's birthplace to Khabarovsk, so they wouldn't have to go to Pobeda and change the birth certificate. I know they just did that for their own convenience. Anya told me to say, however, that I wanted the birthplace kept secret because I wanted the adoption kept secret in Russia. Ridiculous subterfuge—it wasn't worth arguing about, though.

Anya also told me something I had not heard before, at least officially, that Alesia's grandparents were alcoholics. When I had been there in May, the social worker had just said they were too poor to care for her. I don't know how Anya knew that. She was not inclined to share information with me except what was absolutely unavoidable.

After we finished the court prep, two ladies on the orphanage staff made a point of speaking to me about Alesia. Pasha had arrived (while we were prepping for court) to teach his weekly computer class at the orphanage and, after class, he interpreted for me. One of the ladies was a psychologist who works with the kids. She asked me some pointed questions about how Alesia would handle the transition, the importance of talking about feelings, etc. I was somewhat surprised she spoke to me in that way, since the Russians I had encountered so far seemed to think that taking a kid to America would solve all problems. This lady seemed to have a clue about the huge transition affecting Alesia and wanted me to be aware of it. Of course, I had already given it a lot of thought.

Another lady, an older one, also spoke to me. She was one of the few overweight people I had seen in Russia, and had what looked like a fake bun on top of her head, which was sort of comical. She was apparently the supervisor of the caretakers. She talked about how much she cared about Alesia and how much everyone would miss her.

She said something that really touched me—that Alesia had a purity, an innocence, that must be preserved. (I have pondered that statement a lot since then, because it's so true.)

I hated to leave Alesia and go back to the hotel. In the lobby, before she left, Anya said that, because the next day was Sunday, I couldn't see Alesia at all. Anya didn't want to work on Sunday, nor did anyone on her staff. I was dumbfounded. I had flown halfway around the world and I couldn't see Alesia at all the day before court. I wished for the hundredth time I could fire the agency, but they had me—too late to do anything but put up with their rudeness and insensitivity.

As Anya was leaving me at the hotel, she handed me an envelope with some papers in it. When I got back to the room, I pored over them.

The most disturbing thing was an abstract of Alesia's medical records. I wanted the records themselves. All I got was a summary. It said her general health was good but that she was undernourished. I wondered if the orphanage doctor even gave her all the vitamins I had sent. It also said that in school she studied in a "specialized class." I wondered what that meant. I resolved to ask Olga.

The medical report also said Alesia had a "curved nasal septum" and "bile duct dyskinesis in the remission stage." I hoped the doctor in Atlanta could explain that. It sounded ominous to me. Then again, I didn't put much stock in Russian medicals after reading about them on message boards frequented by other adoptive parents.

The next day was depressing, not being able to see Alesia. I spent the morning washing out some things in the hotel bathroom, which was not fun. At least the water wasn't brown, like it was when the choir stayed at the same hotel in 2003. I also sorted through the toys I brought for Svitlana to give to the children.

I had originally planned to take gifts to all the children in Alesia's orphanage and have a party for them all. However, since there were about seventy kids, I revised my plans. I knew I could give Svitlana the extra toys and school supplies and she would see that they got distributed fairly.

Pasha came over at 12:30 and we went to Svitlana's apartment for lunch. We took a hired hotel car. The whole fare to Svitlana's place was about $3. I was glad Pasha was there to help me with the heavy suitcase and speak in Russian for me—he directed the taxi driver to the apartment building.

Like so many buildings in Khabarovsk, the apartment building was really derelict looking on the outside, like a dangerous slum with broken, uneven stairs. The interior corridor was also awful. However, Svitlana had fixed up her apartment very nicely with bright colors, carpet, furniture, etc. The colors were flamboyant—the wallpaper was burgundy in the living room, light blue in the den, silver metallic and blue in the tiny kitchen.

Svitlana preferred to speak Russian rather than English, so Pasha's help was invaluable. I toured the little apartment and we chatted. Then we went through the little toys I had brought. Svitlana had toys everywhere. It was a cozy, kid-friendly place—perfect for a missionary who works with children all the time.

Svitlana gave us lunch, which was a little awkward with the three of us in her tiny kitchen. But it was good. It was potatoes in a kind of gravy and some pork cubes. She also had tea, a small salad, and cookies. We talked about Alesia.

I went back to the hotel after seeing Svitlana and had a half hour rest. Then Olga came over for tea. We sat downstairs in the hotel bar, which was deserted.

Olga was so sweet—she gave me the originals of Alesia's paperwork, drawings, and letters. I had seen e-mails of everything. She also gave me some Russian chocolates. I didn't have anything for her. I hadn't brought the cloth that Mom and I had bought for her and her daughter Zoya. I felt bad at not having anything for her. I did pay her for the remainder of Alesia's lessons, though.

We talked a lot about Alesia, my plans for her education, and how she would adjust to America. Like Svitlana, Olga wanted to know how I planned to help Alesia adjust, where she would go to school, etc. We had a good talk. She left around 5:00.

At 6:00, Toma (Kate's aunt) and Pasha came over and we ate dinner in the hotel restaurant. Toma had wanted me to come over for dinner at her apartment, but I really didn't want to go out at night and make my voice worse. I was still very hoarse.

Toma brought me an old coat of hers, which was pretty nice looking but a little too tight to button. It had some moth holes, but nothing serious. She said, "Just throw it away if you don't want it." She was so funny. We talked in my room after dinner. Pasha had a hard time interpreting for her, because she tended to wander off the subject, but she was delightful anyway. She reminded me a bit of my mother.

I went to sleep about 10:30 Sunday night, but I woke up several times. I had left a wake-up call for 6:30, but didn't need it. I was nervous about the court hearing. My brain felt paralyzed—I couldn't keep a thought in my head for long.

When I opened the curtains in my room that morning, I was greeted with a beautiful panorama of snow. The dingy buildings were transformed. It also looked very cold.

I dressed carefully for court, pulling out my black blazer and good black pants. I wore tennis shoes, but they were black leather and didn't look like tennis shoes. I wore an extra undershirt for warmth and Toma's borrowed coat.

Marina picked me up wearing her usual miniskirt, three-inch spiked heels, and tiny coat. We went to the courthouse and parked right by the door, on the street. No parking problems in Khabarovsk. Back home, one usually must park a couple of blocks away from any courthouse and walk. It was snowing pretty hard.

The courthouse was an older, massive building. It looked pretty much like a lot of courthouses I had seen in America. We walked up a steep flight of stairs to the second floor. There was a big area to check coats. Anya was there. Alesia was there with the orphanage director and social worker. Alesia gave me a big hug. I whispered to her, "Everything will be all right" in Russian and smiled.

Alesia was dressed oddly. She had on tight polyester black dress pants that laced up the side near the cuff, a white shirt with a 1970's looking pointed collar, and a black knit sweater. She wore ugly brown shoes. Her hair was pulled back in an elastic band. She was very poised, though.

The court hearing room was far less scary that I had imagined it would be. However, it had a huge cage in the corner, with a chair and a microphone inside—clearly for criminal defendants. Seeing the cage was somewhat unnerving.

It was a small, narrow room with three rows of chairs at one end and a long conference table in the center. At the other end were a couple of desks and chairs on a small dais. The cage was off to the side.

They provided me with a woman to translate for me, and she was very good. She stood right next to me, and I was in the front row of chairs.

Someone said "All rise" just like in America, and the judge walked in. There were a couple of other ladies at the conference table thing in the middle of the room, and I never got totally straight who they were. The judge was an overweight woman who looked to be about my age. She wore a black skirt and blazer and blouse. She was very stern and spoke very quickly.

They read out the proceedings, Dee Thompson petition to adopt Alesia Pavlova, etc. They asked me to state my name, and I apologized immediately for my voice, which was still hoarse.

Some of the questions were logical, some struck me as almost funny. They asked how Alesia would manage in school, not knowing English. I explained about the intensive ESOL program to help her. They seem amazed that America would educate kids who didn't know English and needed extra help.

The judge thought it was strange that I wanted to adopt a thirteen year-old. She asked me why I didn't want a baby. I explained that, as a single woman, an older child was physically easier for me to manage than a baby. I don't know where that answer came from—it just popped into my head. I hadn't ever really thought about it like that, but it was true.

There was another question relating to why I wanted to adopt a child Alesia's age. I tried to explain that when I met Alesia, I thought she was about seven or eight years old, but the translator didn't get the past tense. The judge kept saying "Don't you realize she's thirteen?" It took me a moment to catch on to why she was confused. I explained about meeting Alesia in January 2003 and how tiny she was. I finally just said, "She needs a mother regardless of her age."

They asked me about Alesia going to college. I said that if she qualified academically and wanted to go, I would send her. I explained about Georgia's Hope scholarships. I didn't mention that they were funded by the lottery.

The judge asked me if I had any experience with children and I said yes, that I had several friends with kids about Alesia's age, and I had spent time with them. I was glad she didn't grill me too hard on that, since I hadn't spent any time recently caring for kids by myself.

Alesia was called in and had to answer several questions. She stood right in front of me. I said a prayer for God to help her. She did great.

The judge asked her if she wanted to be adopted and live in America—she said yes. They asked her when she had met me, and she answered when the choir came to sing at the orphanage. She said she was okay with my changing her name slightly—from "Olesya" to "Alesia." They asked her what she called me, and she said "Dee." This was a little odd since she called me Mama in letters, but I figured maybe she was just nervous.

One of the frustrating things was that there were exchanges in rapid Russian that the translator didn't translate exactly. She would listen, and then say, "The judge is chastising the orphanage director because all the kids aren't in the databank." The judge spent a good bit of time berating the poor woman, but I thought, I hope it causes her to make more efforts to get the kids adopted.

They asked Anya some questions, such as why she wanted Alesia's birthplace changed to Khabarovsk. She said to keep it secret, which I still thought was bizarre.

There was an exchange which was startling to me. The judge asked if they had tried to find Russian parents for Alesia. She asked if Alesia's photo had been published in the paper, and an attempt made to get her adopted by Russians, and they said yes. I wondered if that was true. I was never told about that.

We had to wait about twenty minutes for the judge to decide. I passed the time talking to Alesia. We looked at the drawings and school papers Olga had given me. I learned that the word for butterfly sounded very similar to the word for grandmother. We didn't have any trouble communicating, despite my limited Russian.

Anya and the translator looked at the copy of the photo album and scrapbook I had brought with me. The translator seemed impressed.

The judge returned and it was announced that the adoption petition was granted, and it was over. There was a pause. I grabbed Alesia and hugged her and said in Russian, "I am your mother!" She grinned.

I had expected I would cry, or laugh, or feel something dramatic, but I didn't feel that way—just relieved and happy. The whole hearing had felt sort of unreal—the courtroom was so strange, the language barrier so obvious.

We went back to get the coats. Anya informed me that Marina would take me back to the orphanage and I would be allowed to spend one hour with Alesia. Seeing the stunned look on my face, she said they were busy; they had other clients, etc. It really threw cold water on my joy. I wanted to slap her. This is so unfair, I thought. One hour?!

I got a photo taken of Alesia and me outside the courthouse in the snow. It was the only photo I could get. It was snowing steadily and freezing, of course. Despite that, the world felt new. I had made a family for myself.

On the way back to the orphanage, Alesia and the director sat in the back seat. I told Marina I wanted to take everyone to lunch and celebrate. She said no, that wouldn't be allowed. I sat silently for a moment, resentment welling inside me, spoiling the day. I wanted to shout, I am paying you to help me with this adoption and I am forced to obey you?! The tail is wagging the dog here! Of course, I didn't say that. Marina did agree to take me by the hotel so I could run up to the room and get the final batch of presents I had brought for Alesia.

I tried to make lemonade out of lemons. In the car on the

way to the orphanage, I asked Alesia with Marina translating, "What is the first thing you want to do when you get to America?" she thought about it seriously for a moment, and then said, "I want to see Granny." I said, "What about Uncle Bruce? Do you want to see him?" She grinned and said, "Da!" When I got back to the hotel Monday afternoon I e-mailed Mom and told her that, and copied Bruce. Mom told me later when she saw that she had cried.

When we got back to the orphanage, Alesia spent a good deal of time talking to her friends and running around. She liked the little gifts—lip gloss, craft beads, etc. I also gave her a disposable camera and told her that she could make photos and I would get them developed when we got home. She was delighted with that.

I told Alesia that she needed to make a list of all the girls in her group so that we could have a little party for everyone before she left and give them gifts. I also told her to make a list of the caretakers she wanted to give gifts to—I wanted her to take an active role in the process. I was told there were about eighteen girls, the older ones included. It was so hard to hug her goodbye. I told her I loved her, in Russian.

I got back to the Intourist around 2:00. I wasn't very hungry, so I just bought a couple of pastries in the gift shop and ate those. I was feeling pretty blue—what a letdown after all these months of efforts and prayer. The hearing was easy, really, but now I couldn't see Alesia. I was glad I had decided to return to Atlanta, in a way, because clearly the agency didn't care about letting me spend time with my child. They had their money. I decided then I would never use the agency again if I adopted another child, nor would I recommend them to anyone else.

I went downstairs at 5:30, browsed the gift shops, and

bought a couple of things. Pasha came in, and Larissa and her daughter came right afterwards. Larissa brought a bunch of presents for Kate and her family, for me to carry back for her. We sat and talked in my room for a while. Pasha was good about translating.

When they left, I was very hungry. Pasha and I had a nice dinner at the Korean restaurant downstairs in the hotel. He was so easy to talk to, and he felt much more like a friend and a younger brother. He wouldn't let me pay him for all his help. He did admit he would like me to bring him some tee shirts with American sayings on them.

Going to Moscow that night was a really long plane ride. Nobody around me spoke English. I sat three rows from the bathroom, which again was really stinky and dirty. The two teenagers sitting next to me did not stop talking for seven hours. By the end of the flight, I wanted to strangle them. I suppose it would have been worse if they had been speaking English. I kept trying not to cough. I couldn't get comfortable. The Russian guy in front of me had his seat tilted back so far that I could barely move. He had to sleep off all the booze he drank after he got on the plane.

After nine hours of misery, I got to Moscow. I spent the night in a hotel next to the Moscow airport, grateful to sleep in a real bed. I had a hot shower. The next day, it was back to Atlanta. I was so glad to get home. I missed Alesia so much, though.

Chapter Eighteen

THE HOME STRETCH

The days between trips were very busy.

I got in late Wednesday night. I was jet-lagged all day and felt yucko, but went into work Thursday anyway. I worked all day Friday, and on Saturday went in again for several hours.

Two days on an airplane will flat out make your cold feel much worse, I learned. I lived on Advil Cold and Sinus. I felt slightly stoned, very tired, and emotionally on autopilot.

On Sunday, there was no rest for me. I had to do laundry—it was piled on the floor under my dining room table. I had to pay bills. I had to finish packing. I did some basic cleaning around the condo.

Late Sunday afternoon, I finally went into Alesia's room, flipped on the light, and looked around. The beautiful new blue quilt was on the bed. The stuffed animals were sitting carefully in front of the pillows. The carousel music box was on the dresser, alongside the butterfly coin bank. I had carefully put everything I thought was cute and girlish looking in there. I picked up the stuffed elephant and rubbed my face on his soft ears. I pictured Alesia there and smiled.

I talked to Patty R that night for a long time, and we had a good chat. She told me about some of Snezhana's behaviors when she first got home, like exploring everything in her little world (light switches, microwave, dog) and rearranging her room until 5:00 a.m. the first night.

Patti also said Snezhana had refused to put on her seatbelt at first and that there had been a forty minute standoff, but Patti won. (Kate later said Russians are told that seatbelts are actually dangerous.) I had only seen Alesia in a car once after the court hearing, and she had not worn a seatbelt. I thought that might be a concern, but decided I would cross that bridge soon enough.

I was curious to hear about Snezhana's reactions to her new home, but also felt somewhat detached. The idea of Alesia living in the condo with me still seemed unreal, despite everything. My mind could not make the leap to imagine day-to-day life with her. I was too overwhelmed with the thought of the long and difficult trip to bring her home.

When the plane back to Russia took off on Tuesday morning, I was sitting next to Ricky, thinking about nothing in particular, and chewing Trident gum. We had to wait to board at the last minute because we were flying on Delta buddy passes, so that had preoccupied me all the way to the airport, in the car, checking in bags, and then finding the gate.

I watched the ground fall away as the plane took off and it suddenly struck me—I am going to get Alesia. I am really going to get her and bring her *home*. Tears came into my eyes, and I tried to wipe them away quickly. More came. I tried to hide behind Ricky's newspaper. Finally, I put it down, placed my head in my hands, and wept. Ricky was puzzled—I tried to explain to him about my sense of relief and how I felt, but I couldn't, really. My little girl was coming *home*! My heart heard those words over and over, like a mantra.

In Moscow, we took a taxi to the other airport—the one for the domestic flight. We had three hours between flights, and I was nervous. We found a taxi driver. I said to him the name of the other airport (in Russian), and asked about the fare. The taxi driver wanted $200! The next one wanted more. We finally found one whom we bargained down to $100—by refusing to pay $200. Ricky said let's just sit and wait, and they will come down off that price, and he was right. I was going nuts to get out of there, but Ricky was right.

It was a struggle getting the bags into the taxi. Like most European cars, it was small. We each had two big bags plus a carry-on. The taxi was hot, the trip uncomfortable. At one point the driver just veered off the road and drove on the shoulder for a while. Ricky and I both dozed off and on. Moscow was dirty in the mantle of old snow, and the outskirts we were riding through were mostly ugly, industrial wasteland panoramas. We finally got on our flight to Khabarovsk. Ricky slept. I mostly read a book.

When we got to Khabarovsk Thursday morning, the airport was dark, dirty, and crowded, as usual. I was so tired after no sleep and was like a zombie. Marina was nowhere to be seen. A tiny little man with a wizened face, looking like a Chinese peasant, helped us get the bags, and I tipped him a couple of dollars.

Marina finally arrived. No miniskirt, this time. Marina was dressed in a skintight leather outfit and looked like a dominatrix, or an extra in a Marilyn Manson video. Ricky, a typical male, thought she looked charming. I was irritated with her being so late.

As soon as we walked outside the airport, the wind knifed at us. I could tell Ricky was shocked by the cold. Getting the bags from the airport terminal to the car across the icy pavement (about fifty yards), was brutal.

I was informed by Marina that even though it was Thursday morning, I would not be able to see Alesia until late Friday afternoon. I was furious, but too tired to argue with Marina. Obviously they didn't care about my feelings or Alesia's feelings. I had told

Alesia I would see her on Thursday, and she was counting on it. I couldn't even call the orphanage to tell her I'd be there Friday— I didn't know the number. There are no phone directories in Russia. I should have called Olga to call the orphanage, but I just wasn't thinking straight, after two days with no sleep. I later learned that Alesia had been so upset, she had called Olga, frantic that something had happened to me.

When we reached the Intourist hotel, we checked in and they took our passports—standard in Russian hotels. They register you with the police as a foreign visitor.

I went to my room and tried to nap. Ricky, I learned later, went across the street to the upscale sporting goods store and bought a hat. He had thought he would only need earmuffs. I had told him he would need a hat, but he didn't understand until he felt the Russian cold.

I took a shower and was so thrilled to be clean. I tried to sleep, but I couldn't nap. I got a call from the hotel clerk saying I had to go downstairs, see the manager, and pay for our rooms up front. I didn't understand why. You cannot argue with Russian hotel clerks, though, and win.

I finally just got up, dressed, and went downstairs. After paying for the rooms, I found Ricky. We had a very nice, tasty lunch at the Korean restaurant downstairs. Ricky ordered a lot of hot food. He seemed to feel no jet lag, which was infuriating— of course, he had slept the whole way. I was still tired, crabby, and hoarse.

After lunch I went to see the hotel manager, Natasha. She was very nice. She helped me to arrange for Sunday's going away dinner at the hotel. I wanted to invite all my Russian friends in Khabarovsk, so Alesia could tell everyone goodbye. Larissa, Olga, Svitlana, and Pasha had been so sweet to me. The whole multicourse dinner, including dessert for nine people, wound up only costing a couple of hundred dollars.

With nothing else to do, Ricky and I went shopping late Thursday afternoon. I had to buy gloves. I had lost my good gloves, somehow. I think they were lost somewhere in an airport on the first trip. Gloves are essential in Russia in November.

We got a taxi to take us down to one of the stores on the main street. It was fun to browse, despite the guards with guns everywhere in the upscale store. I bought some souvenirs. I found some nice leather, lined gloves for about $28. I also went ahead and bought a hair dryer. The ones at the hotel were awful—it took forever to dry my long, thick hair. The little dryer only cost about $10.

We started walking back to the hotel—it was sooooo cold, and getting dark. I could feel my cheeks burning from the cold. My throat felt very scratchy, too. I needed water. I was carrying a bottle in my purse, as always.

We ducked into a little shop to get warm and let me re-hydrate. I looked around and realized it was Andre's shop. When the choir had been there in 2003, we had found many lovely souvenirs there, and a nice man named Andre had spoken fluent English and interpreted for us. Andre came over. I shook his hand warmly. Andre smiled, pleased to see me. Andre said he remembered me and the choir.

I was walking to the door, thinking we needed to get back to the hotel, when Pasha walked in. I laughed to see him so unexpectedly. I gave him a hug. The story he told was comical. I had e-mailed him from the USA about getting in Thursday morning. After he got off work, he had gone to the hotel to find us. The hotel desk clerk said we had taken a taxi to the store—they had recommended it. He walked to the store. They told him everything we had bought, and that we were walking back to the hotel. He started walking back, looking into shop windows. He knew Andre and decided to stop and see if we were in there. Obviously the Americans could not go anywhere incognito in Khabarovsk!

I needed to see Kate's aunt Toma and get back Kate's suitcase so that we could take presents to the orphanage in it. It also had my wrapping paper and scotch tape in it. (I was told not to put wrapped presents in luggage, as they would be unwrapped in customs.) So Pasha called on his cell phone and found out where she lived.

We then took a taxi to her apartment, but it was very difficult to locate her building. There were no street signs and no building names. A holdover from communist times, I was told—nobody wanted to be too easy to find. Finally, we found it. Pasha and I went up to Toma's apartment and left Ricky in the taxi. She wanted me to stay for dinner, but I just said I was exhausted and needed to get back to the hotel—which was true. She gave me a lovely book about Khabarovsk for Alesia.

We came back to the hotel and had dinner in the Red Room downstairs (the hotel restaurant). Ricky and Pasha got along well, which was nice. Afterwards, we went up to my room and talked, and Ricky and I both gave Pasha the American tee shirts we had bought for him. Pasha seemed delighted with all the shirts. Anything American is prized there.

I was so tired that I could hardly talk, my throat was hurting, and I was coughing. I had to tell Pasha and Ricky goodnight or pass out. I said goodnight. I had slept little on Monday night at home, had almost no sleep Tuesday night on the plane, and no sleep on the overnight to Moscow on Wednesday—I was too uncomfortable. Despite the hard little twin bed, I was thrilled to close my eyes. I finally slept.

Friday was the most momentous day of my life—I finally
got my daughter! Marina picked us up around noon. We went to
an office and filled out some paperwork to get Alesia's passport.
The woman was very nice. She congratulated me and we chatted
(with Marina translating). It was the second time I got teary-eyed,
when she said "Now you are a mother, congratulations! I wish
you good luck."

We next went to a really nice, American-style grocery store
to buy supplies for the going-away party at the orphanage. I was
amazed. I had been to two other Russian grocery stores on my
trips, but they were quite different—everything was in glass cases,
customers couldn't touch anything. This upscale store was
different. It was just like an American store—you could touch the
merchandise and there was a big variety. The only big differences
were the coat check area as you walked in the door and the many
armed security guys in suits carrying guns and walkie-talkies. We
also ogled the Russians walking around inside in fur coats. It was
so warm inside that we had to take off our coats and put them in
a separate buggy. We got four highly decorated cakes and juice to
drink. Little plastic cups were only sold in packages of two each.
We put everything in Marina's car.

Marina didn't think it was a good idea for Ricky to go to the
orphanage with me. I was so irritated. She said it was against the
rules, since he wasn't my husband or father, they could get in
trouble, etc. I finally said, "Well if they say anything, he can just
wait in the car." Aaargh! How ridiculous. The orphanage people
don't care who goes in there— particularly "rich" Americans. I
said a prayer that everything would go smoothly and that Ricky
wouldn't get kicked out. I really wanted to film the going-away
party.

Ricky and I had a late lunch at the Korean restaurant again.

I had chicken noodle soup. My throat was still so sore, and I was still hoarse. The soup was soothing to my throat. After lunch, we went our separate ways for a couple of hours. I wrapped gifts for the caregivers, then checked e-mail in the business center.

It was dusk when we got to the orphanage, so we couldn't really film outside. We got all the way in the door before Alesia came downstairs to see me and hug me. It was too dark to film, but no matter. She hugged me hard, and I looked down into her excited little face and thought, "Yay!! Finally!"

The kids were excited to see us. They helped us carry everything upstairs. Ricky took a lot of video. He passed out candy and gifts he had personally brought to the kids.

Marina and Alesia and I used the schoolroom to make up the gift bags for each child, while the party table was arranged outside. We had forgotten to buy napkins or paper towels. It took time to fill each gift bag. We stalled by having the girls sing songs, and I played some Simon Says with them. We got along great despite the language barrier. One of the older girls knew some English, which really helped.

We had fun eating cakes and drinking juice. I told the girls how much I liked them, and how much I appreciated their care and friendship for Alesia. They sang a little song they had composed for Alesia, a farewell song. They were so cute and sweet. I wished I could take them all with me.

When it was time to leave, Alesia had to get dressed. She couldn't take any clothes from the orphanage. Marina and Alesia and I went back in the bedroom. She tried on the sweats I had brought and the pants were too short—way too short. I felt awful. Alesia shrugged—didn't seem to care. She was delighted with the coat and new matching pink hat and gloves.

I thought Alesia would be teary at leaving her friends, but

she wasn't. She kissed and hugged everyone goodbye, then headed for the car. She had one small bag of possessions with her—everything she had in the world fit in that one small plastic shopping bag. The many gifts we had sent her were all left behind for the other girls. I know she didn't have to leave everything. She has such a generous heart.

Pasha had come in and joined us at the party, and we gave him a ride back to the city. The car was pretty crowded, but we were fine.

We got to the Intourist and Alesia looked around with great curiosity. She had never seen a hotel lobby before. When the tiny elevator stopped and we got in, she looked around, eyes wide, and held my hand. I knew she was thinking, "Wow! An elevator!"

Alesia was delighted with the hotel room, the bathroom, everything. She explored—which didn't take long in the tiny room. She had never been in a hotel room before. She turned on the water in the bathroom. She looked out the window.

We went to dinner at a restaurant Pasha suggested, and invited him along. When the taxi left us on a dark street, we couldn't find the restaurant entrance for a few minutes, which was sort of anxiety-producing. There were few streetlights and it was quite dark and forbidding. Finally, we found the restaurant. It was a very Russian restaurant, wooden walls with paintings of Russian nobility on the walls. The choir had been there in 2003, I remembered.

Alesia sat right down and started looking at the menu. I looked too—it was in Russian and English. After a few minutes, I had Pasha ask her if she had ever been to a restaurant. She said, "No." Pasha told her how to order. She seemed right at home. She ordered a salad, pilmeni, and dessert. I had pilmeni. Ricky had a steak. The food was very tasty.

When we got ready to leave, I was counting out the tip. Alesia said something to Pasha and I asked him to translate. He grinned and said, "She wanted to know why you were leaving money on the table and I told her it was a tip. She said she had seen that in movies."

When we got back to the hotel, Pasha came in and translated while I had my first chat with Alesia as her mother. I told her that, in America, we bathe and wash our hair every day, and we only wear clothes for one day, then we wash them. We brush our teeth every day. We talked about how to use a shower. I pantomimed how to wash in the shower. Pasha translated faithfully and tried not to laugh. I figured she had not used a shower before.

Pasha talked softly to Alesia for a few minutes. He told her about what it's like to be the only child of a single working mother. His tone and manner with her was so sweet, like a big brother. He was trying to reassure her, and she listened intently. I was so grateful to him. He's a remarkable young man.

When Pasha left, Alesia got in the shower. When Alesia got out, her hair was a rat's nest of tangles and I had a tough time getting a comb through it—she hadn't really understood that she could use the shampoo, I later learned. She had taken a long time in the shower. When I went in later, I found out why. She had washed out her shirt and her panties and hung them up to dry. I wanted to cry when I saw that.

I will have to confess something here. I guess every parent goes through it. There was an odd moment that first night, when we got back from dinner and Pasha had left. I looked at this child who was nearly as tall as I and whose feet were the same size as mine, and thought, Oh my goodness, what have I gotten myself into?! Here I am, sharing a room with someone who doesn't really speak English, and she is my child now. I'm responsible for a whole person, a nearly grown person. I had not thought about this part, this mother part—except in the abstract. Cold terror seized me for a moment.

I took a deep breath, asked God to remove the panic, and it vanished. I looked at my daughter. I'll never forget the sight of her in her pink Hello Kitty pajamas, jumping into the little bed, arranging the duvet and the pillows, clean and with a full belly—obviously just delighted with everything. I walked over and looked down at her shining face. I leaned down and kissed her goodnight and told her I loved her, in Russian. She answered back, "I love you", in English. Thank you, Olga, I thought silently.

A few minutes later, I was lying in bed trying to sleep. I pondered the long journey to get to this place. So many tears, so many frustrations. So many people who cared and helped, though. I had made new friends, both Russian and American. Everyone was interested in hearing about Alesia. Everyone I spoke to knew children who had been adopted, but none as old as Alesia.

Now, I thought, I'm on a new journey, being a mother — this new journey of a thousand miles had now begun with one step—my telling Alesia at the orphanage, "Pashlee" (let's go). Despite all the books I had read, I felt inadequate to be a mother. I pondered the task ahead of me with cold dread. Finally, I just asked God to see us both through this and went to sleep. For the thousandth time, faith sustained me, giving me a peace of mind I could never get otherwise.

Our flight to Moscow didn't leave until Monday so we had the weekend to explore Khabarovsk.

The next morning, I woke up at 3:00 a.m. and couldn't get back to sleep. My cold had worsened. I was coughing more and my head was stuffed up. My throat was very scratchy. I dozed, wrote in my journal, and finally got up and showered at 5:45.

Alesia said she was hungry when I got out of the shower. The restaurant didn't open until around 8:00. So I gave her a Snickers bar. Probably set a bad precedent, but, so be it, I decided. The child was hungry. I always bought Snickers bars when I found them, in Russia, because I never knew when it would be impossible to find snacks.

At 7:30, we got Ricky and went down to breakfast. They opened up early for us, which was nice. Ricky and I got the American breakfast. Alesia got the one that was basically yogurt, bread, a mixture that looked like coleslaw, and juice.

After breakfast, we went back up the room and called my mother. I knew she wanted some reassurance that I had Alesia and all was well. Alesia said, "I love you!" to her, in English. We chatted briefly. I could hear the relief in her voice.

After buying Alesia some blue jeans at a store recommended by the hotel, we went back to the grocery store and found snacks to keep in the room, so I didn't have to feed Alesia any more emergency candy bars. We bought Russian chocolates, too, for gifts. Ricky bought Alesia some flowers, which was sweet. I knew he missed his kids. He talked about them a lot.

We came back to the hotel and put away our purchases. Then we walked several very long, freezing cold city blocks up to the new cathedral, snapping a lot of photos along the way. It was very beautiful, but so biting cold. Alesia skipped along, wearing her long underwear, sweatpants, and heavy insulated coat, hat, gloves. She was obviously oblivious to the cold.

The Russian Orthodox cathedral was very new, and

gorgeous. Ricky was disappointed when he went in with his camera and was told not to take photos—an emphatic hand gesture from a large unsmiling Russian man. It was gorgeous inside, but they sold icons and trinkets just inside the door, which made it less church-like, to me. There was a bride in there, in white, but there was no wedding party, no vows, people were just milling about. I didn't know why. Their wedding customs must be quite different.

We left there and walked across the street to a Chinese restaurant with an excellent all-you-can-eat $4 buffet. I couldn't identify many things, but that may have been good. The food was good. Definitely more Russian/Chinese, though. Alesia tried all the many salads, and ate several chunks of raw tomatoes. She only ate a little meat. She drank cups of hot tea.

After lunch, we spent a pleasant couple of hours going through the Khabarovsk museum. It was the kind of place where, when you checked your coat, they made you put little cloth booties over your shoes. I guess that was to protect the marble floors and expensive rugs. They had some gorgeous, ancient-looking Chinese vases. There were many icons and paintings from the 1400's and older. In every room, there was a stout matron sitting on a chair, making sure nobody got too close to anything or touched anything. There were some paintings and statues of nudes, which Alesia ignored. I was amazed—at her age I would have giggled with great embarrassment at all that statuary nudity.

We got back to the hotel around 3:00 and rested. Alesia read a Russian teen magazine. Ricky had persuaded me to let her buy it at the grocery store. It looked just like an American magazine, but in Russian. She also colored with some markers and paper I had brought. I then showed her my Walkman, which she loved. She happily listened to it for a long time afterwards. She tried all the CD's, but liked James Taylor best. She has good taste.

Pasha came by around 5:00 and went to dinner with us. We had dinner at the Japanese restaurant upstairs. The food was good. We were the first ones there, thanks be to God, so there was less cigarette smoke. Alesia ordered shrimp, but when it arrived, she looked dismayed. She asked Pasha in Russian, "Is this the foot of something?" We all had a good laugh about that.

The next day was Sunday. We went to the circus in the afternoon. It was very European. One ring, some acrobats, some trained bears and cats, and clowns. Not thrilling, but interesting. We didn't think to ask Alesia before we went if she had ever been there before. I had just assumed she had never been to the circus. When Pasha asked her, she said she had been twice—once just this past October. She looked mildly interested in the acts and more interested in her popcorn.

After the circus, we caught a city bus downtown. It was so freezing cold while we were standing outside waiting on that bus. I had never experienced that kind of cold and I thought, I'd endure 5 minutes in hell just to get warm. The entire bus fare for all four of us was about $1. It was collected after we got on and sat down by a woman who came around. The bus was about half the size of American ones. Two Russian guys on the bus had on American clothes with logos—one was Columbia Sportswear. It was so incongruous to see American clothes there.

Pasha took us to a downscale Russian mall that looked like an indoor flea market. Tiny little stores, very limited stock, but many stores. We found Alesia another pair of blue jeans, which she needed. We next went looking for dress shoes for her to wear to the little party that night. She didn't want anything with a heel—though the Russians love spiked heels. We finally found a pair of nice shoes, brown leather mules. They won't look too weird in America, I thought.

We got back to the hotel about 6:00, and hurriedly dressed. I had scheduled the little going away party for 7:00. I got Alesia dressed for the going away dinner in a beige corduroy skirt and a white turtleneck, plus the blue beads I had bought her at the museum. The transformation was astonishing. The little orphan was gone and she looked like a young lady. Both Ricky and Pasha noticed.

All my Russian friends showed up. I had prearranged the menu. We had a little salad with fruits and some veggies—like a waldorf salad, but no nuts. Then we had a dish of some sort of like crepes filled with crab and cheese. The main course was pork chops with a sort of sauce of tomatoes and mushrooms and, on the side, what I called Russian tater tots. An artfully arranged slice of cucumber was on each plate. For dessert there was an elegant parfait of vanilla ice cream with fruit garnish. We just drank water and juice, and Ricky had a coke.

After everyone sat down and started eating their salads, I had a coughing attack so bad that I had to run up to the room and swig down some cough medicine. That was embarrassing. I was coughing so hard I sounded like I was dying, and I was afraid I would wet my pants. I was afraid the hotel would call an ambulance to take me away to the TB ward of the local hospital!

After the dinner and more visiting up in the room, more gifts were exchanged, speeches, etc. All the ladies were very emotional. I was exhausted. I finally sent everyone home in cabs, so they wouldn't have to catch buses at night in the cold.

Alesia enjoyed the dinner. At the the end, after everyone left, though, she said, "I'm tired." I didn't have to persuade her to go to bed.

The next day was our last in Khabarovsk. We ate breakfast, packed, and checked out, but the hotel let us store the baggage there for the day. We left and walked around town, shopping. I bought Alesia a couple of books in Russian. Finally, late that afternoon, we went back to the hotel and got our bags, and the agency rep was there to take us to the airport —a young man, one I had not seen before. He was very quiet.

Pasha was there at the airport to see us off. His help was invaluable. We had to get our luggage wrapped up in plastic (a Russian requirement because they abuse the baggage so badly). There was a little stand that wrapped bags, and charged $3 or thereabouts. Pasha supervised the wrapping. He also helped talk to the airline people about our passports. It was nerve-wracking because we barely got all the bags wrapped and had to get to the front of the line to check them, since we were running late for the flight. There was a lot of tension.

When Pasha left us, he hugged everyone goodbye. It was sad. His face showed great concern. I will never forget it. I didn't know what he was worried about, really. Alesia told me much later that he had seen her crying. I didn't see it—probably a good thing.

We had to wait for the plane in a dark, smelly area with people smoking nearby and broken booze bottles on the floor— a typical bus station waiting area in America would be much nicer. Alesia seemed fine. I was very tired and irritated, and my throat hurt. Ricky kept finding people to talk to in broken English.

It was an easy flight. Alesia played with her handheld translation device, listened to the Walkman, and generally entertained herself the whole time. When the plane took off, it was dark, so she couldn't really see the land falling away. She wasn't frightened. I looked down at the lights of Khabarovsk and thought, Thanks be to God. I never have to go back there! I want to be home.

Chapter Nineteen

ALESIA IN AMERICA, FINALLY

We got into Moscow Monday night around 8:00. With the eight hours time difference, it felt like the middle of the night to me. Anatoly (the agency rep) met us when we landed in Moscow. The ride to the hotel was long and uncomfortable. Alesia got nauseated. Anatoly had some car-sickness pills and gave her one. She wanted to hold her head near the open window of the car. I nearly froze from the draft. It took an hour to drive to the hotel.

I liked the Hotel Ukraina. It was elaborately decorated and very old. The room was enormous—high ceilings, wood wardrobe and table. The lobby was huge—five restaurants, several gift shops. We ate a late dinner at one of the restaurants.

The next morning, despite only getting about six hours' sleep, we had to get an early start to get to the American embassy. As instructed by Anatoly, Alesia and I got up early and met him downstairs at 8:00 a.m. after a quick buffet breakfast. The buffet was quite nice, and I even ate a couple of fried eggs—real eggs, not powdered. I also drank some delicious pear juice.

Anatoly took us to a doctor who apparently does a lot of examinations of Russian children being adopted by Americans. His office was in a campus-like place not far from the hotel, in a reasonably decent looking building. It was extremely cold and snowy, however.

The doctor spoke English fairly well. I stayed in the room, of course. The doctor did part of his exam—the part where he thumps the abdomen—while Alesia was standing up, which was odd. He listened to her heart, talked to her, etc. He said to me in good English that she was 5'0" and weighed eighty lbs. Her health seemed to be fine, although she was malnourished. He also said that she needed to get some exercise, preferably swimming or dancing. Her little arms and legs were like sticks. He gave me a paper listing the immunizations she had had, and said they were the same ones she would have had in America. The sheet was in English, which surprised me.

The doctor made one remark which I found irritating: "You only have to worry about the boys in a couple of years. She is a beautiful girl." I felt like saying, listen, jerk, in a couple of years the boys will have to contend with ME! But I didn't see any reason to chit-chat about it. Alesia was given some immunizations by a nurse, then a chest x-ray was done. She had to have that for the embassy visit to prove she didn't have TB, since she had been exposed to it. She handled everything calmly.

We left there and went to the embassy to take care of some paperwork. We parked outside on the street and trudged through the dirty snow to the front of the line. Anatoly spoke to a guard and we were shown in. That's why I had paid extra to get his help.

At one point, I had to write out a translation of the parents' marriage certificate because the agency had not had it translated in Khabarovsk. Anatoly sat and read the translation and I wrote it down on the back of the form in English. I was surprised they let Anatoly do that, but I knew he knew the folks at the embassy.

While I was writing, it struck me as incredibly sad—these are Alesia's parents. These people got married on Valentine's Day, six months after Alesia was born. I looked at Alesia sitting nearby, as she blithely ignored everything but her handheld Yahtzee game Ricky had given her, and I thought, How could they give this beautiful little girl up? How could her father leave her when she was just a baby? How could her mother just let them take her away a few years later and never even try and see her again? I got big tears in my eyes. It was so awful and sad.

When we got back to the car and started back to the hotel, I felt this odd mixture of emotions. I just started crying. I couldn't help it. There was an overall feeling of deep sadness that this beautiful little girl had to go all the way to America to be loved by a proper family. I also felt this huge wash of relief that the whole ordeal was almost over. Anatoly kept saying, "Why are you crying? Everything is fine." I couldn't explain. I finally got it under control and said to Alesia in Russian, "I am okay, I am just very tired and I don't feel good." I hated crying in front of her. She kept leaning up from the back seat and patting me.

We got back to the hotel and my thoughts turned to more mundane matters. We turned in some laundry to be washed—it was only about $4 and the maid took care of it once we filled out the list. Ricky had gotten some stuff laundered the day before and said that they had done a good job.

I didn't want to go out to lunch with it being so cold and raw outside, so we ate in another hotel restaurant. At noon, Russians are not ready for lunch. So we were the only ones in the elegant restaurant. The food was again expensive—$75 for the three of us. Moscow is a very expensive place to stay.

The embassy interview that afternoon was pretty dull. The room was filled with babies, with only a few older kids. I chatted with several parents.

My embassy "interview" was a young guy who asked me a few easy questions through a window, like a teller's window. I said that, yes, we would have health insurance; she would learn English at school, etc. These were the same questions that everyone else got, I knew. I apologized for my voice, which was still hoarse, and he said, "All the parents get sick here, don't worry about it." Must be a combination of the cold and damp, and terrible pollution, I thought. He handed me a sealed packet of documents to give to the customs people in New York, and that was it.

We came back to the hotel and checked e-mail. I sent off an e-mail to Mom and Bruce about the events of the day. I got a surprising e-mail from Bruce asking about Alesia's favorite colors, and if she might like a backpack with her name embroidered on it. I re-read it twice to make sure I wasn't delusional from the jet lag. I finally thought, what a change! He now really believes she's my child. I almost cried again, but I didn't. I had hoped and prayed all along he would come around. I knew the transformation had started when he had given me the money.

Alesia and I had an early dinner at the buffet restaurant downstairs. It was almost 9:00 and I was headed to bed. I was so happy to have the bureaucratic paperwork all over except for the foreign ministry registration, which Anatoly was handling. I thought, now we can relax and sightsee for a few days.

The next morning we had a good breakfast, then toured the Kremlin. The tour cost over $100, but I got a private guide and car. The hotel helped me arrange it. The guide, a college girl named Tatiana, did a great job explaining everything in English and Russian.

I had toured the Kremlin's impressive churches and museum with the choir in 2003, but now I saw it with new eyes. This was my daughter's heritage. Alesia skipped around and seemed interested in everything, but didn't seem overly impressed by the history. I got goose bumps standing in a church that was over 1,000 years old and held the crypts of patriarchs (Russian orthodox popes). Tatiana patiently explained everything to Alesia in Russian. She said that Alesia didn't know much Russian history.

The wind was raw and was spitting snow the whole time. I feared that I would slip and fall on the wet pavement or the outside staircases, which had no railings.

We got to go through the Armoury, where the Tsar's treasures are stored. Alesia didn't seem all that impressed with the royal robes, crowns, suits of armor, fabulous priceless china, etc. I was fascinated. We had to rush, though, because we only paid Tatiana for three hours.

On the way back to the hotel, Ricky announced that he needed to go back to Atlanta to take care of some business. The more I thought about it, the more I realized my plan of staying in Moscow until Saturday to sight-see was very unappealing. I felt sick and I couldn't get medicine for my cough. The weather was awful, and Alesia seemed blasé about Moscow in general.

I called Anatoly and he said he could expedite the foreign registration—for an extra $130. I knew he had bribed somebody. I didn't care. I just wanted to be home. I changed the travel arrangements with relief.

We had dinner in the hotel. By 9:00 p.m. I was packed and ready to leave. I spent a restless night, coughing and coughing. I felt so bad about being so loud, but Alesia slept through it all.

The next morning, Anatoly picked us up at the hotel and we headed to the airport. At one point, we had to re-route because Putin was headed to his office and the entire route had to be cleared of traffic. Anatoly headed off on a circuitous route, cursing the traffic.

When we finally got on the nice big Delta jet and Alesia realized we were making the flight to JFK in business class, her eyes got really big. "Kraseevah!" she exclaimed (awesome). She was thrilled with the video screen, video games, the little cosmetics pouch, the lovely attention of the flight attendants—

including the one named Lisa who spoke Russian with her—and
she didn't sleep a wink. For ten hours. Nor did I, but I can never
sleep on planes.

After going through customs in New York, we walked
through the airport like zombies. I knew Alesia was overwhelmed
by the enormous place and I was concerned about keeping her
calm. Ricky had slept on the plane and was rested and jovial.

Since we were on buddy passes, the flight to Atlanta was in
coach, not business class.

We landed in Atlanta and I was so relieved to see Maria and
her son. Alesia had slept all the way from New York, as had Ricky.
I had stayed awake, sniffling and crying a bit, so glad to be going
home. I was accepting the transition to motherhood in stages, and
still very emotional.

When we got to the condo, Alesia took a quick look at her
room, then flitted around the condo. Ricky and his family stayed
a few minutes, then left. I realized I was starving.

Alesia's first meal in America was at Waffle House, about
9:30 p.m. It was close, open, and the menu had pictures of the
food. She ate two fried eggs, sunny side, toast and grits. I didn't
have to tell her, she just ate them. She's a southern gal now, I
laughed. I also made her try a bite of waffle and she admitted,
"etta f'coosnah" (it's yummy).

After dinner, we hugged Maria and Perrin goodbye; she had
been so sweet to pick us up. When we went back to the condo
and they had left, Alesia explored more, winding up the music
boxes, examining the dolls, trying on clothes, and opening all the
dresser drawers. I finally persuaded her to get a shower and we got
to bed about midnight.

The next day was Friday. We slept almost twelve hours,

before finally getting up around 11:00 a.m. I took Alesia grocery shopping, and we watched some TV. I wanted to keep things low-key.

Saturday was a momentous day.

Mother and Bruce came over from Augusta on Saturday morning. I was still sick and jet lagged, but so happy to look out the window and see the blue Highlander. "Alesia, Granny and Uncle Bruce are here!" I told her, in Russian. She went out and flew down the stairs.

The minute she saw Alesia, Mother grabbed her and hugged her and started crying. I wanted to cry, too, but fortunately I was so tired and filled with cold medicine that my normal reactions were blunted.

It finally seemed real, though. Really real. All my life, things had not seemed real to me until I saw my mother's face. Once I saw little Alesia in my mother's arms, then it was finally and truly real. I felt such an odd mixture of relief, love, happiness, and sadness that it had taken so long...

Alesia's Uncle Bruce gave her a huge stuffed dog and a beautiful red backpack with her name embroidered on it. He also took her to walk, tickled her, and hugged her several times. I thought, with relief and joy, he is going to be a doting uncle.

I looked at Alesia with these two people who loved her so much and I thought, Thanks be to God. Home at last with my beautiful daughter! It was all worth it. God granted me my miracle. I am a mom.

THE END

Afterword

When I started the adoption, I had great doubts about my ability to ever complete it. It seemed like such an impossible goal. The fact that I could, despite so many obstacles, finish the adoption, was a miracle. I feel strongly that it was only with God's help that I have my daughter home today.

Alesia has been home for over four years now and is doing great. We've had some challenges, but nothing I couldn't handle. She sees a therapist who helps her deal with the abandonment and sadness in her past. She does well in school now, after I learned she has a learning disability and got her therapy for that. She makes friends easily. She speaks English with only a slight accent. She helps me around the house. She is the joy of my life.

In 2005, my mother moved to Atlanta and we bought a house together. It's a spacious house in a nice middle-class neighborhood. Alesia helps me plant flowers, plays in the yard, and swims at the neighborhood pool. I am so glad my kids have a yard they can play in, and we do a lot of gardening.

Emotionally, Alesia is somewhat behind her peers. She is catching up, though. Physically, she has gained over thirty pounds, has grown 5 inches, and is very healthy.

Shortly after she came home, I decided that I didn't want Alesia to grow up without siblings. I adopted a little 10 year old boy from Kazakhstan in 2007. Alesia is a wonderful older sister to him, and I feel my family is complete. My children are totally bonded to me. We share a lot of laughter.

Before my son came home, Alesia helped me write a children's book called Jack's New Family, to give my son some insight into how it feels to be adopted. It's in Russian and English. Many families who have adopted older children have written me to tell me how much they like the book and what a valuable resource it is both for parents and their children.

Despite new, stricter requirements, hundreds of children are adopted every year from Russia, mostly by Americans. The paperwork requirements vary, depending on the region. It doesn't have to be an 18 month long ordeal like my adoption. Most of the children adopted from Russia and other foreign countries are babies. Only about 5% of adoptions are of older children, that is, children older than 2 years old. For most children over age 5, they will never be adopted.

One reason I wrote *Adopting Alesia* is because I hope my story will inspire single women to create their own families, instead of waiting for Mr. Right. I also hope to inspire people to adopt older children.

I write a blog called The Crab Chronicles, and it gives readers a pretty accurate picture of daily life with my two children. Their issues are very much like those of biological kids.

You can find my blog here:
http://deescribbler.typepad.com/my_weblog/
I hope you will check it out.

Thanks for reading and sharing my journey.
Dee Thompson
Spring 2009

SPECIAL THANKS

There were so many people, Russian and American, who were instrumental in making Alesia's adoption a reality, and I want to thank them here. They all have enriched my life enormously and I will be forever grateful to them for their kindness and friendship.

Danny Griffin is no longer affiliated with the church in Ohio, but he and his wife are now living in Belgorod Russia and teaching English there. He has a small non-profit ministry called Soldiers of Christ Ministries, Inc. He says: "We are assisting people in need throughout the world. We give money to Svitlana for ministry. We help orphans, send money and aid to persecuted Christians in India. The money also helps us minister to people by providing us insurance, travel, literature, as well as other needs. We get no salary from the ministry." Donations can be sent to: Soldiers of Christ Ministries, Inc., 15022 SE Territory Drive, Clackamas, Or 97015.

Svitlana Mayboroda is still ministering to more than 700 orphans in Khabarovsk. You can donate to her ministry by contacting her at svitlanamay@gmail.com. Her website is http://www.o4c.org/.

Tomara Shuiskaya and Larissa Lopatina are still in Khabarovsk. They were so kind to me when I was in Khabarovsk. Toma was wonderful about delivering letters and packages to Alesia. I will never forget their kindness.

Olga Volnycheva now lives in Oregon and is teaching English there. Her talented daughter Zoya did the illustrations for my children's book, Jack's New Family.

Kate Humphrey still lives in the Atlanta area, and is a busy Russian interpreter and translator. We stay in contact and are still good friends.

My friend Pasha (Pavel Shokorev) is an engineer and lives in Khabarorsk. He calls us occasionally. I hope he will visit one day.

Photos

First Photo of Dee & Alesia

Nadia & Alesia

Alesia in the orphanage, with presents from America

Olga, Alesia, and Svitlana at the going away dinner,
Alesia's last night in Khabarovsk

Alesia & Pasha

Dee's Family & Alesia

Printed in the United States
218263BV00004B/1/P